WELEX TRAINING

WELEX TRAINING

Stratigraphic Traps in Sandstones
—Exploration Techniques

The Association gratefully acknowledges
publication support in the form of a loan from the
Michel T. Halbouty Fund of the AAPG Foundation.

Memoir 21

WELEX TRAINING

Stratigraphic Traps in Sandstones —Exploration Techniques

by DANIEL A. BUSCH

Published by

THE AMERICAN ASSOCIATION OF PETROLEUM GEOLOGISTS

Tulsa, Oklahoma, U.S.A., July 1974

In memory of my son,
Daniel Andrew Busch

(Jan. 21, 1942–Dec. 5, 1966)

contents

foreword

This book presents a modified version of a 12-hour lecture series on sandstones which has been presented before 55 geological audiences. Most of the presentations were given under the auspices of the Continuing Education Program of The American Association of Petroleum Geologists. This volume was prepared because numerous individuals from these audiences have requested material from these lectures. Although this book contains much information that is not new to geologists associated with petroleum research laboratories, comparatively few exploration geologists have access to the reports of such laboratories. This report should be of particular benefit to explorationists who work for small companies or independents, and to geological consultants not in a position to pursue research actively.

Published data on both modern and ancient sediments are reviewed briefly, and are supplemented by ideas and examples developed by the writer in his practice as a consulting geologist. No attempt is made to review any article completely. Instead, only those aspects are reviewed which pertain to the internal and external features of reservoir sandstones that have direct practical application to oil and gas exploration. Hypotheses and theories of origin of sandstone bodies are reviewed where necessary in order to provide sufficient background for a better understanding of discussions of the methods of oil exploration.

The bibliography at the end of the book is divided into seven categories. It is not complete; however, it includes sufficient references relating to each type of sandstone to be of considerable help to any geologist who wishes to study a particular type. Very few textbook references appear in the bibliography because most of the ideas expressed here do not appear in such texts.

I have benefited greatly from numerous informal discussions with various members of my audiences. I am particularly indebted to Arthur A. Meyerhoff and Peggy Rice for their review and constructive criticisms of the manuscript, and to Deborah Zikmund for her careful editing. I also thank Kathryn Meyerhoff for drafting. I am grateful to Mr. and Mrs. Howard Clark for numerous photographic reproductions of the illustrations used both in the lectures and the text. I also thank John R. Warne for a photograph of his plaster model of a meander belt.

DANIEL A. BUSCH
Tulsa, Oklahoma
March 1973

1

introduction

The practice of modern subsurface exploration geology requires a knowledge of the fundamentals of stratigraphy. To acquire this background, the petroleum exploration geologist must have mastered the basic principles of mineralogy, sedimentary petrology, sedimentation, stratigraphic paleontology, and geomorphology. Although these subjects generally are taught as separate disciplines, they nevertheless overlap and are interrelated. A working knowledge of all these subjects is germane to understanding the problems of subsurface stratigraphy. Areas within these disciplines which merit particular emphasis are: principles of deposition, depositional environments, stratigraphic time markers, and stratigraphic and paleogeomorphic traps.

A treatment of the principles of deposition is inherent to a basic course in sedimentation. These principles are applied to a wide variety of energy environments, each of which must be considered separately to determine the type of sand body that might be deposited. A broad classification of energy environments includes four major areas of deposition: terrestrial, lacustrine, marginal marine, and marine. Each of these comprises numerous contrasting energy environments in which abundant clastic sediments accumulate. Table 1 is one classification of depositional environments.

There is much literature describing Holocene deposits formed in most of the environments listed in Table 1. A moderate amount of literature describes ancient counterparts of these environments based on outcrops. However, very little has been written about the identification and delineation of these ancient counterparts in the subsurface. Therefore, this treatment of sandstones outlines, and provides examples of, methods of subsurface stratigraphic analysis. Consideration is given to the problem of identification and use of the lithologic time marker. Judicial use of the lithologic time marker makes it possible to (1) identify the type of sand-

1

Table 1. Classification of Depositional Environments

   I. Terrestrial
      A. Floodplain
      B. Channel
      C. Dune
      D. Alluvial fan
      E. Talus
      F. Glacial

  II. Lacustrine

 III. Marginal marine
      A. Coastal plain
      B. Beach
         1. Foreshore
            a. Barrier beach or offshore bar
         2. Backshore
      C. Chenier and chenier plain
      D. Bay and lagoonal
      E. Tidal flat
      F. Tidal sand bank
      G. Deltaic
         1. Birdfoot
         2. Estuarine
         3. Arcuate
         4. Cuspate
         5. Lobate

  IV. Marine
      A. Continental shelf
      B. Continental slope, continental rise, bathyal, and abyssal
         1. Turbidite
            a. Channel (submarine canyon)
            b. Submarine fan
            c. Basin floor

---

stone body, (2) relate its geometry to its depositional environment, and (3) predict its subsurface development beyond that which can be determined from the available control data.

Detailed study shows that a high percentage of the trap-forming sandstone present in the subsurface is in either stratigraphic or paleogeomorphic traps. Both types of traps are identified and analyzed best in the subsurface by relating them to lithologic time markers. Also, both types are known to be abundantly productive of oil and gas. It is safe to predict that the vast majority of the future reserves of oil and gas in continental North America will be found in these two types of traps.

The principal tools available to the subsurface stratigrapher consist of a combination of cable-tool and rotary sample cuttings, cores, and mechanical logs. The principal types of logs are electric, radioactivity, and acoustic, although more than 30 types of mechanical logs are used. It is imperative that the exploration geologist be thoroughly familiar with all of these tools.

A deliberate attempt is made to select subsurface examples from all parts of the stratigraphic column and from numerous sedimentary basins. Thus, it should be apparent to the reader that the principles and methods discussed have application to petroleum exploration problems throughout the world.

EARLY METHODS OF PETROLEUM EXPLORATION

Petroleum exploration, like any other "art," has undergone a series of evolutionary changes insofar as geology has been applied to it. When geologists first applied their specialized knowledge of the earth's crust to oil finding, their main effort was directed to stratigraphy and structure of outcrops. Numerous sections were measured, described, and plotted in detail. One or more key marker beds were identified and surface structure maps were constructed for the purposes of leasing and drilling.

It soon became apparent to surface geologists that cable-tool drilling operations furnished a whole new dimension to their efforts. For the first time it was possible to know, rather than to speculate, what the nature, depth, and extent of numerous formations might be. This new knowledge was available through the medium of microscopic examination of the sample cuttings. Entire formational units having no surface manifestation were identified and mapped for the first time. By projecting and correlating outcrop stratigraphy with subsurface stratigraphy, it became apparent that most of the strata presently exposed at the surface were deposited in ancient marginal-marine shelf environments. Because of the prevailing conditions in marginal-marine areas, unconformities are most abundant in sedimentary units of this environment. Separate unconformities near the seaward edge of a depositional shelf (hinge line) characteristically converge, and even merge, in the direction of the shoreline. The multiplicity of thinner strata, the converging unconformities, and the abundant facies changes in the shelf environment of deposition were not fully understood until subsurface sample data became available.

In the early 1930s, mechanical logs were introduced to the petroleum industry, and for the first time the exploration geologist had a precision tool to measure accurate depths, thicknesses, *etc*. It was then possible to correlate lithologic character, based on sample determinations, with electric-log configuration, based on spontaneous potential and electrical resistivity of the various formational units penetrated by the bit. More sophisticated mechanical logs have been introduced to the industry over the years. Combinations of these logs, supported by plotted sample descriptions, are used in establishing precise subsurface stratigraphic correlations. From this combination of data, very meaningful structure maps have been constructed for areas where there is little or no surface indication of folds or faults. Isopach maps of various types of stratigraphic units can be constructed from these sample and mechanical-log data. It is even possible to construct structure and isopach maps of rocks below unconformities in areas where the outcropping formations give no hint of the true subsurface conditions.

Grabau (1913), in his *Principles of Stratigraphy,* established the concept of lithofacies relations. It was Krumbein (1945, 1948) and Dapples *et al.* (1948), however, who demonstrated that lithofacies maps clearly reveal the geometry of depositional basins and the geographic spread of major lithologies for arbitrarily selected stratigraphic units. These works constituted the first really meaningful approach to quantifying and portraying graphically what previously had been just an abundance of descriptive stratigraphic data. The techniques were applicable to both surface and subsurface data, and the two could be used together. This approach represented quite an advance from the use of conventional isopach maps, because ratios and percentages of contrasting lithologic types could be illustrated graphically to establish depositional trends favorable for the accumulation of oil and gas. Such maps are especially useful in connection with basin studies and regional stratigraphic analyses. However, they are of very limited value in establishing specific drillable prospects.

Within the past 10–15 years, there has been an increasing awareness among petroleum exploration geologists that all sedimentary rocks are the products of their respective depositional or epigenetic environments, or both. Many sedimentary rocks, particularly sandstones, have a geometry which is directly related to the paleodepositional environment. Thus, the shape, size, and trend of an individual sandstone unit are in many cases genetically related to the paleogeomorphology. This whole relationship is well developed by Martin (1966). Another pertinent reference on this subject is the AAPG publication *Geometry of Sandstone Bodies* (Peterson and Osmond, 1961). Both references are strongly endorsed for use by petroleum exploration geologists as examples of more recent trends in thinking.

PERTINENT SOURCES OF INFORMATION

The growth of the science of subsurface stratigraphy has been distressingly slow, considering its importance to the petroleum industry. There appear to be three principal reasons for the slow development of subsurface stratigraphic analysis.

First, the authors of most university textbooks seldom have an opportunity to delve extensively into the problems of subsurface stratigraphy. Most geology professors concerned with stratigraphic research direct their attention to outcrop stratigraphy rather than to subsurface stratigraphy. Thus, their emphasis generally is petrologic or paleontologic. Very few academicians have access to abundant subsurface data, and still fewer are interested in such problems.

A second reason for the slow development of basic concepts of subsurface stratigraphy appears to be a general lack of background knowledge in the concepts of such disciplines as sedimentation, stratigraphic paleontology, and geomorphology. This observation applies particularly to most petroleum exploration geologists. The solution to this problem appears to be continuing self education.

A third reason is that the opportunities for publication by well-trained oil-company researchers commonly are restricted by company management. Much of the worthwhile investigation in this field is being conducted in perhaps a half dozen petroleum research laboratories. The findings generally are presented in confidential company reports and are not released to the trade journals for publication until any competitive advantage has been realized. A wide variety of significant geologic research projects is being pursued in major-company petroleum research laboratories. Some are long-ranging fundamental research projects which can be classified as basic research, whereas others offer the possibility of more immediate practical application.

A very important source of information pertinent to subsurface stratigraphic problems is the literature on Holocene sediments. There has been a very significant upsurge in such studies in the post–World War II period. Several North American research organizations have conducted extensive work on Holocene sediments; among them are the Scripps Institute of Oceanography, Woods Hole Oceanographic Institution, United States Beach Erosion Board, American Petroleum Institute, Lamont-Doherty Geological Observatory (Columbia University), United States Coast and Geodetic Survey, Louisiana State University Institute of Coastal Studies, and Arctic Institute of Canada.

Many students of modern sediments are more interested in applying their findings to fields other than that of subsurface stratigraphic analysis. It is the responsibility of the subsurface stratigrapher to ferret out of these studies the material which has potential or immediate application for solving problems in petroleum exploration. In this treatment of sandstones, the writer has borrowed freely from papers about Holocene sediments in an effort to demonstrate the necessity of using data from any and all sources for answers and methods in subsurface stratigraphy.

FUNDAMENTAL CONCEPTS OF FACIES RELATIONS

Most oil and gas produced from noncarbonate rocks is found in reservoir rocks deposited in the marginal-marine environment. Table 1 emphasizes the significance to the petroleum geologist of the various reservoir types that are classified as marginal marine. The marginal-marine environment is one of comparatively high-energy conditions in contrast to terrestrial, lacustrine, and truly marine environments. It is an area in which significant oscillations of the shoreline occur. These lateral shifts of the shoreline may be the result of tidal conditions, tectonic movements, or eustatic changes in sea level—or of all three. Regardless of cause, the lateral shifts of the shoreline in the marginal-marine depositional environment are accompanied by similar shifts in the sites of deposition of distinct sedimentary types. Inasmuch as (1) uniformity in university teaching on the significance of this environment relative to its closely related sediments is lacking, and (2) a working knowledge of the facies relations within this environment is essential to meaningful stratigraphic analysis, it is desirable to review here the fundamental concepts and principles. In a subsequent section these concepts and principles are illustrated by specific examples.

The concepts of marine transgression and regression are considered to be fundamental. The meaning of these terms, however, is not the same to all geologists. In the American Geological Institute *Glossary of Geology and Related Sciences* (Howell, 1960), instead of giving a definition of *transgression*, reference is made to the terms *onlap* and *overlap*. The meaning of the term *onlap* is considered to be the same as that of *transgressive overlap*. In the same publication, the reader is referred to the definition of *offlap* for the meaning of the term *regression*. The statement is made that the term *offlap* is described by some as *regressive overlap*. Clearly, *processes* have been confused with the *results*—the stratigraphic relations result from the processes of transgression and regression. The new AGI *Glossary of Geology* (Gary *et al.*, 1972) does define the terms *transgression* and *regression* as processes, more consistent with the writer's understanding.

In order to simplify and remove some of this confusion, the following definitions of transgression and regression are offered. *Transgression* is the process of migration of a shoreline in a landward direction. *Regression* is the process of migration of a shoreline in a seaward direction. As defined here, these terms may be applied to either a marine or a lacustrine environment. Neither definition implies wedgeout of sedimentary rocks, either toward or away from the depositional basin. Only where the stratigrapher correlates time units and observes that certain sedimentary units have either a transgressive or a regressive relation to the time lines are such terms as *onlap, overlap, offlap,* and *regressive overlap* applicable. Moreover, only from the observation of such physical relations can ancient transgressions and regressions of the shoreline be inferred. The concept of transgression and regression, as determined from the overlapping relations of relatively shallow or deeper water facies, is extremely pertinent to the petroleum exploration geologist because of certain practical and significant factors, among which are the following.

1. Paleogeomorphology of bordering land—Was it a deeply dissected, rugged terrain, a gently undulating peneplain, or possibly a tidal flat?

2. Nature of source of sediment supply—Was it igneous, sedimentary, meta-igneous, metasedimentary, or possibly a combination of these?

3. Paleoenvironments of deposition—Which types existed, and to what extent did they control the trend, distribution, and thickness of sand bodies?

4. Mechanisms of deposition—What sedimentary processes existed at each locale, and to what extent did they predetermine the shape and internal structure of a body of sand?

5. Cause of migration of a shoreline—Were shoreline movements the result of eustatic changes in sea level? If so, the facies would be shifted laterally, either seaward or landward. If, however, shoreline movements were the result of tectonism (*e.g.,* Rocky Mountain uplift during Paleocene time), abundant new influxes of terrigenous clastic sediment and shoreline regression would have occurred.

Other currently less practical, perhaps academic, aspects of geology related to the transgression-regression concept are:

1. Time—How far back in geologic history was a particular sediment deposited?
2. Rates of sediment supply.
3. Dispersal of sediments.

These are some of the more difficult problems related to transgression and regression. The solution to any one of these problems can have a significant application in petroleum exploration.

2

terrigenous deposition in marginal-marine areas

The overlapping and wedgeout relations of the sediments deposited in a marginal-marine embayment can be complex. Everywhere, however, the relations give an indication of the behavior of the surface of deposition—subsiding, rising, or stationary. Also, the relations reflect the nature of the tectonic movement, that is, gradual or cyclic. The rate of sediment supply relative to the rate of submergence or emergence of the depositional surface also may be determined. Table 2 is a summary of important variables affecting deposition in the marginal-marine environment.

The comparisons between supply of sediment and the rate of subsidence, as shown in Table 2 (A1a and A1b), are modified from Grabau (1913, p. 728, 734), who first recognized the interrelations of the two variables. This table also catalogs and systematizes the relation of the supply of sediment type to cyclic subsidence and emergence and to gradual emergence (A2, B1, B2). The existence of predictable cyclic sequences of strata was emphasized first by Wanless and Weller (1932) in coal-measure sections in the Eastern Interior basin. A review of the cyclic sequences of sediments deposited in marginal-marine environments reveals that the principle of cyclic sedimentation applies to deposits dating from earliest Paleozoic time to the Holocene. The extent to which cyclic sedimentation may be related either to cyclic tectonism (rising and lowering of sea bottom) or to cyclic changes in sea level is not known. As a mechanical convenience, the sedimentary patterns illustrated in profile in Figures 1–10 are related to changes in sea level. The same sedimentary patterns would result if sea level had remained constant and the surface of deposition had moved up or down in either a gradual

7

**Table 2. Variables Affecting Terrigenous Deposition
in Marginal-Marine Areas**

A. Sinking bottom
   1. Gradual subsidence
      a. Supply of sediment less than rate of subsidence
      b. Supply of sediment greater than rate of subsidence
      c. Supply of sediment equal to rate of subsidence
   2. Cyclic subsidence
      a. Limited sand supply, abundant mud supply
      b. Moderate sand supply, abundant mud supply
      c. Limited sand and mud supply
      d. Abundant sand supply
      e. Strike-valley sand

B. Rising bottom
   1. Gradual emergence
      a. Limited sand supply
      b. Moderate to abundant sand supply
   2. Cyclic emergence
      a. Steady sand supply

C. Stationary bottom

or a cyclic manner. The vertical exaggeration is great in all of these diagrammatic illustrations.

GRADUAL SUBSIDENCE

Sediment Supply Less Than Subsidence Rate

Figure 1 is a diagrammatic illustration of a sedimentary sequence deposited in a marginal-marine environment in which the surface of deposition is sub-siding more rapidly than sediment is being supplied. As a result, the shoreline gradually transgresses from right to left. Within the area of net transgression, the marine sandstone lies unconformably on continental strata. The several sand-mud lines are "phantom" lines that represent the maximum depth of wave agitation for the several successive positions of sea level that are shown. A high-energy environment characterizes the site of marine sand accumulation above this line. Above this phantom line, wave and intertidal energy is sufficiently great to keep most of the silt- and clay-size particles in suspension. These finer

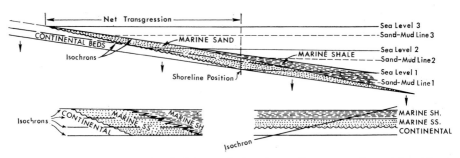

FIG. 1—Sedimentary sequence deposited in marginal-marine environment; surface of deposition is subsiding more rapidly than sediment is being supplied. Modified after Grabau (1913).

particles remain in suspension until they are transported into an environment of lower energy (*i.e.*, protected bay or lagoon), where they settle and form either a silty shale or a clayey deposit. The water below the sand-mud line is essentially quiet. Thus, clay- or silt-size particles in this area settle to form a marine shale that is the time equivalent of the more shoreward marine sandstone. In Figure 1 the supply of sediment is only half that necessary to keep the shoreline in a constant position. This condition may be interpreted to indicate the presence of a low-lying borderland being drained by sluggish streams. The lithologic units (continental beds, marine sandstone, and shale) clearly transgress the time lines (isochrons). The illustration in the lower left of Figure 1 is drawn using isochrons as datums of reference. This is a graphic means of illustrating that the three lithologic units are depositional time equivalents. In the lower right of Figure 1, lithologic boundaries are used arbitrarily as datums of reference. In this portrayal, most of the time equivalence of the several lithologic units is obscured. The chief interpretation shown in Figure 1 is the most probable explanation for the formation of a widespread, blanket-type marine sandstone.

Sediment Supply Greater Than Subsidence Rate

Figure 2 gives an interpretation of a marginal-marine environment in which the supply of sediment to the site of deposition is greater than the rate of subsidence. In fact, the supply of sediment is twice that necessary to keep the position of the shoreline constant. As in Figure 1, the respective sites of marine sandstone and shale deposition are controlled largely by the vertical position of the sand-mud line. The three dominant lithologic types are clearly regressive to the time lines. This relation may be interpreted to indicate that an active neighboring source area at the left is being drained by streams having both

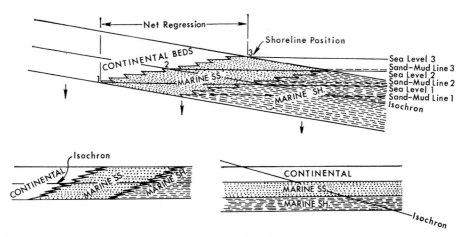

FIG. 2—Sedimentary sequence deposited in marginal-marine environment; rate of sediment supply is greater than rate of subsidence. Sediment supply is twice that necessary to keep shoreline constant. Modified after Grabau (1913).

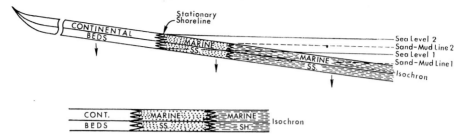

FIG. 3—Sedimentary sequence deposited in marginal-marine environment; rate of sedimentation is equal to rate of subsidence, and shoreline maintains stationary position. Modified after Grabau (1913).

moderate and steep gradients. In this situation the continental (nonmarine) beds are as thick as their marine time equivalents. Isochrons are used as datums of reference in the lower left of Figure 2. This method of portrayal emphasizes both the regressive nature and the time equivalence of the continental beds, marine sandstone, and marine shale. In the lower right of Figure 2, the lithologic boundaries are used arbitrarily as the reference datums. The manner in which the isochrons are "crossed" by the three regressive lithologic units contrasts sharply with that shown in Figure 1.

A comparison of Figures 1 and 2 shows that the stratigraphic sequence in Figure 1 consists of continental beds unconformably overlain by sandstone, which is overlain by shale. In Figure 2 the stratigraphic sequence is completely reversed; the shale is overlain by sandstone, which is overlain by continental beds; unconformities* are absent.

In places where faunal assemblages are directly related to the depositional environment, a lateral shift (either transgressive or regressive) of the site of either sand or mud deposition is accompanied by a similar lateral shift of the fauna, especially the benthos. The net effect is a lithofacies-controlled fauna which may either transgress or regress time lines, or both.

Sediment Supply Equal to Subsidence Rate

Figure 3 illustrates a situation in which the rate of sedimentation equals the rate of subsidence. As a result, the shoreline remains stationary. Because the shoreline neither transgresses nor regresses, great thicknesses of continental beds, sandstones (including reservoir types), and shale units accumulate. An example is the Oligocene Frio barrier-bar system of the Gulf Coast of Texas (Boyd and Dyer, 1964), in which the maximum thickness is known to approximate 5,000 ft (1,525 m).

---

* The types of unconformities referred to in this report are adopted from Dunbar and Rodgers (1957, p. 118–119) and are defined as follows: *nonconformity*—stratified rocks lie on nonstratified igneous or metamorphic rocks; *angular unconformity*—an angular discordance separates two units of stratified rocks; *disconformity*—all the strata are parallel, but the contact between two units is an uneven erosion surface; *paraconformity*—the contact between two successive strata is a simple bedding plane, at which position a hiatus is inferred.

In the situation illustrated in Figure 3, the sandstone and shale units are of the same age, and the transitional zones separating the marine sandstone from the continental beds, on the one hand, and from the marine shale, on the other, are nearly vertical. Bedding planes and time planes are, in effect, identical, and cross the transitional zones at right angles. Very thick marine sandstone sequences must be explained by such a situation in which the rate of subsidence is in equilibrium with the rate of sedimentation.

CYCLIC SUBSIDENCE

Limited Sand and Abundant Mud Supply

A fairly common example of the facies relations which result from cyclic subsidence is illustrated in Figure 4. The supply of sediment is insufficient to offset the rate of subsidence; thus transgression occurs. In this example there are a limited supply of sand-size material and an abundant supply of clay- and silt-size material. In fact, the available sand is insufficient to form a continuous blanket overlying the unconformity. This condition results in a series of beach sands which impinge on the unconformity and wedge out basinward. They bear a vertical *en échelon* relation to each other. The position and shape of each sandstone body shown on Figure 4 are extremely generalized, and each position represents a stillstand of the shoreline in a period of overall marine transgression. The mud and clay sequences separating the sand wedges form as a result of cyclic subsidence (under conditions of limited sand supply) in which transgression is too rapid to permit sand accumulation. The nature of the beach environment of deposition is discussed and illustrated in a subsequent section. Each of the sand wedges in Figure 4 is a composite of the sediments deposited in the upper and lower foreshore environment. Thus, one wedge of sand, as generalized here, may consist in part of beach sand and in part of one or more offshore bars. A vertical series of *en échelon,* thin, discontinuous marine carbonate beds may be present basinward from each of the wedges of sand. In most places these carbonate beds consist of diagenetically altered clastic ma-

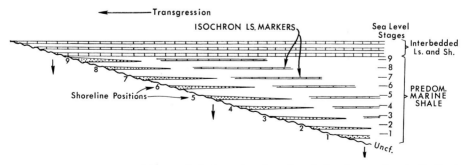

Fig. 4—Cyclic subsidence with very limited supply of sand and abundant mud and silt. Sand wedges impinge against unconformity and represent a succession of stillstands of shoreline in overall marine transgression.

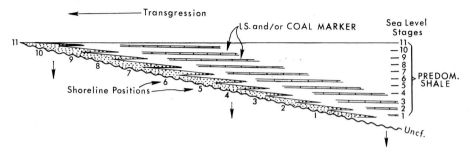

FIG. 5—Cyclic subsidence with intermediate supply of sand and abundant supply of mud. Sandstone blankets unconformity. Upper surface of sandstone consists of a series of *en échelon* wedges, each of which represents a stillstand of shoreline.

terial. The mud and clay sequence separating any two of them generally has a constant thickness, any deviation from which is a slight increase in thickness basinward. The individual carbonate beds are deposited contemporaneously with shoreward sand bodies at the same level. The carbonate beds are very extensive, parallel with the shoreline, and are a few miles to 10–15 mi (16–24 km) wide perpendicular to the shoreline. Thus, they are excellent lithologic time markers for detailed stratigraphic analysis. The uppermost part of Figure 4 indicates depletion of the sand source and shows that the sediments consist entirely of an alternating sequence of thin carbonate beds and mud or clay beds.

An isopach map of the stratigraphic interval from the unconformity to any one of the several thin carbonate beds shown at the top of the diagram would be a simulated reconstruction of the topography prior to the cyclic marine transgression. The irregularities on this unconformity surface directly control the irregularities of the shoreline trend at any stage of cyclic subsidence. This trend, in turn, partly controls the sinuosity of that part of the marginal-marine depositional environment in which sands are deposited. The seaward gradient of this unconformity surface also is a factor in determining not only the irregularities of the depositional trend, but also the variations in width of a particular sand body. Such an isopach map is an excellent tool for tracing and projecting each of the *en échelon* sands in the direction of depositional strike.

Moderate Sand and Abundant Mud Supply

The sedimentary and stratigraphic situation illustrated in Figure 5 is similar to that in Figure 4 except that, in Figure 5, the source area (at the left) furnishes a moderate supply of sand and abundant mud. The mud is interrupted by numerous thin beds of limestone. There is sufficient sand available to blanket the unconformity. The principal evidence for cyclic subsidence is the "shingled" appearance of the upper part of the sand and the *en échelon* arrangement of the thin marine carbonate units which are deposited basinward from the sand wedges. Although there well may be effective porosity and permeability within such a sand body, the body still may contain separate and distinct reservoirs for hydrocarbon accumulation. These reservoirs may develop as a result of either structural or stratigraphic causes. A postdepositional tilt in a counterclockwise direction could cause each of the "shingles" of sand to become a separate reservoir, each having its own oil-water or gas-water contact. In such a situation the main body of the sand, where it lies on the unconformity, could be entirely waterbearing.

The paleotopography at the unconformity can be restored by selecting any of the several thin carbonate beds as a reference datum and constructing an isopach map of the predominantly clay-mud interval from this datum to the underlying unconformity. Because each carbonate datum has only a limited geographic distribution, the use of a "phantom" horizon in areas away from the carbonate bed may be necessary.

Limited Sand, Moderate Mud, and Abundant Carbonate Supply

An example of cyclic subsidence in which there is a limited supply of sand, a moderate supply of mud, and an abundant supply of carbonate material is illustrated in Figure 6. As in Figure 4, separate bodies of beach sand are deposited *en échelon* (as seen in vertical section) along the unconformable slope. Each sand body has a time-equivalent thin carbonate unit present basinward. The beach sands are deposited parallel with successive shoreline positions. The topography of the unconformity surface can be reconstructed in the same manner as for Figure 5; or the top of the carbonate wedge may be used as a reference datum in constructing an isopach map of the interval above the unconformity. The relatively persistent thickness of the predominantly mud-clay interval between the unconformity and the carbonate wedge is the most striking feature of this illustration. This mud interval may extend as a continuous lithologic unit for hundreds of miles both normal to and parallel with the depositional trend.

In an American Commission on Stratigraphic Nomenclature Note (1948,

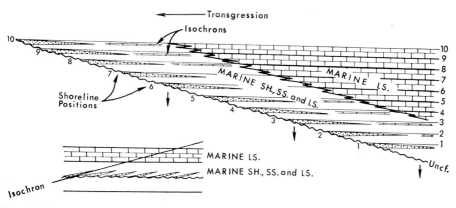

Fig. 6—Cyclic subsidence with limited supply of sand, moderate supply of mud, and abundant supply of limestone. Each wedge of sandstone is deposited parallel with, and adjacent to, successive positions of shoreline.

p. 366), the Geological Survey of Canada defines a sedimentary formation as ". . . a lithologically distinctive product of essentially continuous sedimentation selected from a local succession of strata as a convenient unit for purposes of mapping, description, and reference." This definition refers to a rock unit whose differentiation is not based on time relations. The predominantly mud-clay unit of Figure 6 is clearly transgressive in relation to the time lines; all of the unit is older on the right side of the time lines shown on this illustration. Most of the contained marine faunas have the same pattern of distribution. The interpretation shown in Figure 6 is derived from the Lower Silurian stratigraphic sequence of the westernmost part of the Appalachian geosyncline. Although the dominant source of sediments in this basin is believed to have been on the east, it is also demonstrable that the northeast-trending western margin of this narrow embayment transgressed generally northwestward. The successive "shingles" of beach sand deposited along this northwestern shore clearly indicate the cyclic nature of either the subsidence of the depositional surface or the rise of sea level. The shale and sandstone illustrated in Figure 6 belong to the Clinton Formation; the limestone wedge is the drillers' "Big Lime" (Siluro-Devonian). The thin limestone members, arranged vertically en échelon in the Clinton shale, are referred to by drillers as "packer lime." They are lithologic time markers and are useful as reference datums in selective isopach mapping of parts of the Clinton shale that underlie these datums.

The Chattanooga Shale is another example of a marine shale unit of fairly uniform thickness which is transgressive of time lines. It contains Late Devonian fossils at its type locality in Chattanooga, Tennessee. It has been traced northward 400 mi (645 km) along the east side of the Nashville dome and across Kentucky into central Ohio along the east side of the Cincinnati arch. It is a continuous lithologic unit. In east-central Ohio this shale is of Early Mississippian age and is underlain by the Bedford Shale and Berea Sandstone (earliest Mississippian). The Chattanooga Shale is a transgressive unit of Devonian age toward the southwest and Mississippian age toward the northeast.

From the two cited examples, it appears that any marine shale which maintains a uniform thickness for a considerable distance in a direction normal to shoreline trends is likely to have either a transgressive or a regressive relation to the time lines.

Abundant Sand and Mud Supply

Figure 7 shows an example of cyclic subsidence under conditions of abundant sand and mud supply. The sand forms a continuous transgressive blanket lying unconformably on either marine or continental beds. Although generally great, the thickness of the sand varies considerably. Time lines are transgressed conspicuously by the sand blanket. Two distinct types of lithologic time markers are shown—thin limestone and thin black shale. The latter is the better marker to use for a reference datum in this instance because it is more extensive. Black shale markers may extend into nearshore sandstones (Fig. 7). Such thin units

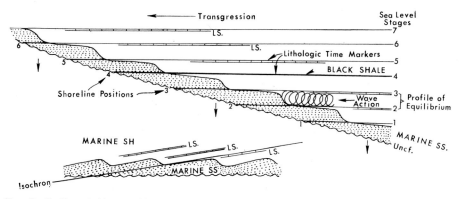

FIG. 7—Cyclic subsidence with abundant supply of sand and mud. Sandstone is a continuous, thick blanket lying on unconformity. Terraced upper surface is interpreted as result of wave erosion and deposition during successive stillstands of sea level.

of black shale produce a characteristic "pip" on the resistivity side of the electric log.

The irregular profile of the upper surface of the sandstone is interpreted as the result of wave erosion during successive stillstands of sea level. This erosion produces a series of sand ridges which are steeper on the seaward side. A post-depositional counterclockwise rotation of this section would produce ideal traps for accumulation of oil and gas along the highest parts of the individual ridges. In order to map the structure of the upper surface of such a sandstone body, abundant well control is required. Thus, this type of map would have very little exploratory value. It would be extremely helpful, however, to be able to predict the positions and trends of the individual terraces (or ridges) and to determine whether they are rotated in a counterclockwise direction.

Such predictions can be made by selecting a lithologic reference datum, such as the thin black shale, and measuring the vertical distance either down to or up to the top of the sandstone. When these measured values are contoured, the resulting map simulates the submarine paleotopographic surface of the sandstone. A structural contour map, constructed on a transparency, may be drawn with the reference datum as a base and then be superimposed on the paleotopographic map. Use of this combination of maps helps the exploration geologist to outline prospective areas for oil and gas accumulation.

Strike-Valley Sands

Figure 8 illustrates a stratigraphic situation which is difficult to classify systematically according to Table 2. Although this would be an example of cyclic subsidence (A2e), it also can be classified logically under gradual subsidence, where it would appear as "A1d." In this example, the unconformity underlying the sandstone bodies controls their trend and distribution. This unconformity is an erosion surface on a tilted sequence of alternating limestone and shale. The result is a series of subparallel escarpments and strike valleys. The escarp-

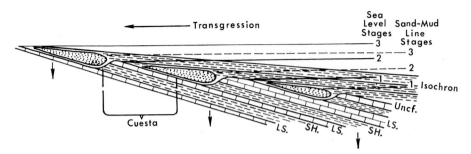

Fig. 8—Cyclic or gradual subsidence where asymmetric "teardrop" lenses of sandstone are deposited in strike valleys developed between escarpments on old land surface. Sandstone lenses terminate abruptly seaward and thin gradually landward. They may be extremely elongate and may be parallel with strike valleys in which they are deposited.

ments are sustained by rock that is resistant to weathering and erosion, whereas the strike valleys are present where subsequent streams have cut into less resistant strata. The subsequent streams are tributary to consequent streams, which were the first streams to develop on a newly uplifted land surface. Because lenticular sandstone bodies later occupy the strike valleys, it is logical to postulate that some cross-trending sandstone bodies occupy the consequent stream valleys. Such sandstones should have similar angular relations to the strike valleys, because the consequent streams flow nearly at right angles to the trends of the subsequent streams.

The sandstones in the strike valleys may be described as having an asymmetric tear-shaped profile (Fig. 8). They thin gradually toward land but terminate abruptly seaward. They may be many miles long. A shale section several feet thick generally separates the individual sandstone bodies from the underlying unconformity surface. This shale may represent a reworked soil profile. Because the several sandstone bodies of Figure 8 have an *en échelon* arrangement with respect to each other, it is mechanically convenient to classify them under the heading of "cyclic subsidence." However, the same arrangement of asymmetric, subparallel sandstone bodies probably could result from gradual subsidence under conditions of limited sand supply. The energy factors causing such an arrangement of sandstone lenses are not certain. It is assumed that the sand is derived from the upland area (left of Fig. 8). It is assumed further that longshore current and wave energy kept the land-derived silt- and clay-size materials in suspension, whereas the coarse (sand-size) materials settled into the lagoonlike area between two adjacent escarpments. Wave base inside one of these lagoonlike embayments is likely to be shallower than in a normal marginal-marine area where waves are free to pound on a beach. Where two escarpments isolate a lagoonlike area, the more seaward escarpment ultimately is submerged by the marine transgression. The vertical position of this crest relative to sea level controls effective wave base.

The lithology and structure below the unconformity are very important in determining the type of sand body that is deposited along the margin of an advancing embayment. The strike-valley type of sandstone, although elementary in concept, generally is difficult to recognize in the subsurface.

Strike-valley sandstones are, in reality, a specialized type of channel sandstone. Although they occupy valleys formerly eroded by subsequent streams, the fact must be kept in mind that two subsequent streams may flow in opposite directions, either away from or toward each other, into the master consequent streams, or stream, to which they are tributary. Thus, they can occupy different parts of the same strike valley.

Because strike-valley sands are most likely to be deposited subparallel with the trace of an ancient shoreline and are elongate and lenticular, they can be misidentified easily in the subsurface as fossil offshore bars. Criteria for distinguishing strike-valley sands from offshore bars are given in a subsequent section.

In Figure 8, the truncated sequence of limestone and shale beds dips seaward. Thus, the first (oldest) strike-valley sand deposited (on the right) lies on the youngest part of the stratigraphic sequence below the unconformity. Conversely, the youngest of the three strike-valley sands shown lies on the oldest part of the stratigraphic sequence underlying the unconformity.

Figure 8, as well as Figures 1–7, is diagrammatic, and its purpose is to portray fundamental concepts. Many more illustrations could be added, most of which would be modifications of those discussed and illustrated here. For example, a sand type similar to, but not identical with, strike-valley sands could be deposited over selective parts of an unconformity surface where the truncated strata were dipping away from, rather than toward, the embayment. In such a case the strike-valley sands should wedge out abruptly landward and thin gradually seaward.

Another modification of the strike-valley concept would be the case of an abundant supply of sand during gradual subsidence. Depending on the rate of sediment supply versus the rate of subsidence, either a transgressive or a regressive blanket of sand could be spread over the entire unconformable surface. Thus, instead of isolated biconvex lenses of sandstone, a blanket sandstone with an asymmetric "washboard" base and a flat upper surface would result. Under conditions of cyclic subsidence, with a moderate to abundant supply of sand, the resulting sandstone body would have an asymmetric "washboard" base and an *en échelon* arrangement of sandstone wedges interfingering with shale at the top. Between these rather distinctive upper and lower surfaces would be a solid blanket of transgressive sandstone. From these few modifications of basic sandstone types, it is apparent that many more combinations can exist in nature.

Gradual Uplift

Limited Sand and Abundant Mud Supply

Figure 9 shows the situation where the surface of deposition is rising gradually and sand supply is limited. Under these circumstances, shore deposits

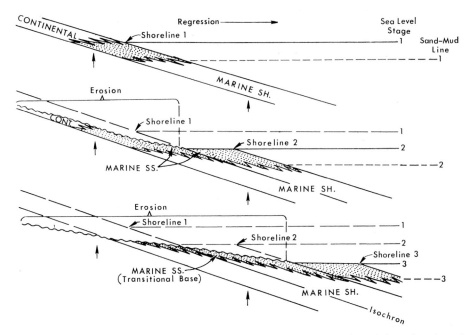

FIG. 9—Gradual uplift with limited sand supply. There is continuous erosion of shore deposits and recycling of marginal-marine sands deposited in regressive sea. Basal contact of sandstone is transitional with underlying shale, and upper surface is partly unconformable and partly conformable with any sediments deposited later.

are destroyed progressively and the sandstone and shale facies are regressive. In Stage 1, a marginal-marine sand is deposited in the area from the shoreline to the line of intersection of the sand-mud line and the submarine depositional surface. The result of weathering and erosion of the sand and continental beds under conditions of gradual emergence and limited sand supply is shown in Stage 2. The upper surface of the sand and continental beds (shown in Stage 1) is an unconformable surface in Stage 2. Furthermore, the shoreline has retreated (regressed) to a new position. The eroded material of Stage 2 is transported to the margin of the embayment, where the sand is separated from the silt and clay by wave sorting. Thus, the marine sands and continental beds of Stage 1 are recycled in Stage 2. In Stage 3, all continental beds and most of the marine sand of Stage 1 have been eroded. Furthermore, the new sand of Stage 2 is actively weathered and eroded. The site of sand and mud deposition gradually has shifted farther seaward. The basal contact of the sand is transitional with the underlying mud. A part of the upper surface is disconformable, and the seaward part is conformable. In all three stages, lithologic types cross the isochrons.

As a result of this combination of gradual emergence of the depositional surface and limited sediment supply, the marine sand body deposited has a very limited width but may have a linear trend of many miles. If the surface of deposition should begin to subside, the lenticular sand body shown in Stage 3 would be completely isolated because of mud deposition above it. This complete isolation of such a sandstone lens in shale would offer ideal conditions for hydrocarbon entrapment. Such conditions existed in many areas of the Gulf Coast during the Cenozoic.

Moderate to Abundant Sand and Mud Supply

The facies arrangement resulting from conditions of gradual emergence combined with a moderate to abundant sand and mud supply can be visualized by reference to Figure 2. Although this figure is discussed as an example of gradual subsidence in which the rate of sediment supply exceeds the rate of subsidence, it is also applicable to this situation. The source area of the sediments and the site of their ultimate deposition are uplifted concurrently at similar rates. Figure 2 is the only example known to the writer for which it might be difficult, if not impossible, to determine whether the depositional surface was submerging or emerging. In such situations, a correct analysis generally can be made by determining whether the stratigraphic sequences just above and below were deposited during submergence or emergence, because the intermediate stratigraphic unit is likely to represent the opposite condition.

CYCLIC UPLIFT

Moderate, Steady Sand and Abundant Mud Supply

In some places cyclic emergence of a depositional surface occurs. Figure 10 illustrates the facies relations resulting from cyclic emergence where the supply of sediment is steady and moderate in quantity. The overall picture is that of a regressive sheet sandstone bordered on the seaward side (right) by marine shale and on the landward side (left) by coal and continental beds. This sandstone differs, however, from the type shown in Figure 2 in that there are localized areas where it is thick. Each area of locally thick sandstone represents a stillstand of the beach environment as the shoreline regressed in a cyclic fashion. The areas of thin sandstone between the locally thick sandstones are due to fairly rapid regression. The thickness of this sheet sandstone is related directly to the rate of regression and the amount of sand available. The dashed

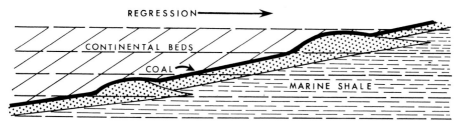

FIG. 10—Cyclic uplift with moderate, steady sand supply. Each area of locally thick sandstone represents a stillstand of beach environment. Sheet sands represent relatively rapid regression of shoreline.

horizontal lines in Figure 10 are isochrons. Each crosses, and thus illustrates concurrent deposition of, four lithologic types, from left to right: continental beds, a coal-forming swamp, marine sand, and marine mud. In this situation, where the coal bed overlies a regressive marine sandstone, it cannot be used as a datum for subsurface stratigraphic analysis. The reason is that it was deposited in a narrow fringing swamp which regressed and then transgressed with the continental and marine environments. Under the conditions illustrated in Figure 10, the locally thick sandstone is likely to have well-sorted sand grains, better porosity, and better permeability than the thin sheet-sandstone beds. The sheet sandstone is not well sorted, is thinner bedded, and may even be interbedded with shale.

Stationary Bottom

Deltaic Sequence

Figure 11 illustrates the facies relations resulting from a stationary depositional surface. The arrangement of the facies is independent of the rate of sediment supply. The successive positions of the regressive shoreline are numbered

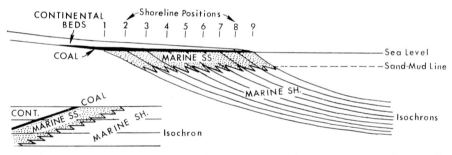

Fig. 11—Stationary surface of deposition with steady supply of sediments resulting in regression of shoreline. This sedimentary sequence is fairly typical of a deltaic environment. Tilt of foreset beds is greatly exaggerated for a marginal-marine delta. Isochrons are concave upward and have a regressive relation to all four lithologic types illustrated. Modified after Grabau (1913).

to emphasize the direction of movement. Because there is progressive basinward thinning of the shale beds, the time planes are curved. The coal bed separates the continental beds from the underlying marine sandstone and, as in Figure 10, cannot be utilized widely as a reference datum. The conditions shown in Figure 11 are fairly typical of deltaic deposits, but are greatly oversimplified. Topset, foreset, and bottomset beds are normally developed. Under marginal-marine conditions, however, none of these beds are likely to be deposited with such steep dips as are shown in Figure 11; the attitudes of the foreset beds are especially exaggerated. Steeply tilted foreset beds are formed only under very restricted conditions, which are discussed and illustrated in the section on deltas.

The lower part of Figure 12 is a duplication of Figure 11. It is presented to illustrate some of the normal complexities which may confront the subsurface

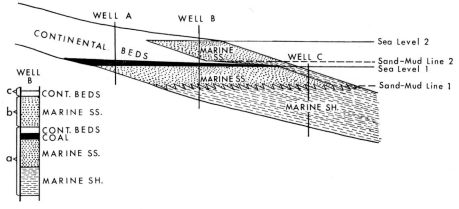

FIG. 12—From base upward: (a) stationary surface of deposition with regression of shoreline; (b) rapid subsidence that exceeds rate of sediment supply, with transgression of shoreline; (c) stationary surface of deposition with regression of shoreline.

stratigrapher when he compares the logs of various wells. In the example, three wells were drilled through sedimentary units that are in sharp contrast but, nevertheless, are genetically related. Well A encountered a preponderance of continental beds underlain by a much thinner section of coal and, below that, marine sandstone. In well B, a more variable stratigraphic section with a partially repetitious sequence of strata was drilled. Well C penetrated a preponderance of marine shale interrupted by a thin marine sandstone. Reconstruction of the depositional history, as seen in this profile, shows the following sequence: (a) stationary bottom with regressive sediments (Table 2, C); (b) subsidence greater than the rate of sediment supply (A1a); and (c) stationary bottom with regressive sediments (C).

EXAMPLES OF FACIES RELATIONS*

Grabau (1913, p. 738) early recognized the transgressive-regressive nature of the Cambro-Ordovician sedimentary sequence in the Appalachian geosyncline. Figure 13 is a northwest-southeast cross section of these strata. Sandstone X-Z is transgressive and represents the Reagan equivalent. Time lines 1–5 (numbered on right) impinge progressively against the upper surface of the "Reagan" and emphasize the transgressive origin of this formation. Formation X-Y represents the St. Peter Sandstone, which is both regressive and transgressive. The regressive aspect is illustrated by the manner in which time lines 6 and 7 impinge successively against the base of this sandstone. The stratigraphic interval between the "Reagan" and St. Peter sandstones is occupied by the Beekmantown dolomites. These dolomites were deposited under both transgressive and regressive conditions. The St. Peter Sandstone (X-Y) is overlain by the Black River carbonate rocks, which represent a transgressive sequence that thins northwestward. The

* Grabau's (1913) work provided the basic material for this section.

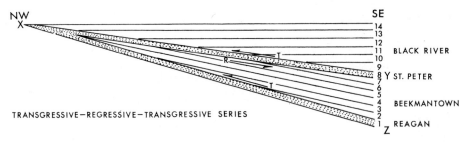

FIG. 13—Diagrammatic cross section of Cambrian-Ordovician sedimentary sequence in Appalachian geosyncline. Modified from Grabau (1913). "Reagan Sandstone" is transgressive, whereas St. Peter Sandstone is both regressive and transgressive. Time lines 1–8 are parallel with each other but are not parallel with time lines 9–14.

successive impingement of time lines 9–14 against the upper surface of the St. Peter illustrates the transgressive nature not only of the upper part of this formation, but also of the Black River. The St. Peter Sandstone (X-Y), because it is first regressive and then transgressive, must contain an intraformational unconformity. It is probable that most of the regressive phase of the St. Peter was eroded before deposition of the transgressive phase. This erosion would have produced a pronounced unconformity at the top of the Beekmantown, such as that known in Ohio. Calvert (1962, 1963) clearly illustrates the progressive northwestward truncation of the Beekmantown as the Chepultepec and Copper Ridge Dolomites have been progressively removed in this direction.

Time lines 9–14, although parallel with each other, are not parallel with those of the Y-Z (2–7) sequence. This lack of parallelism between the two groups of time lines illustrates that two distinct genetic sequences of strata are present.

If the regressive stratigraphic interval (time lines 6–8) is separated from the Y-Z interval, the presence of a third genetic stratal sequence is apparent. From Figure 13 it should be obvious that a detailed stratigraphic study of the Cambro-Ordovician sequence of the Appalachian geosyncline involves dividing the section into distinct, genetically related combinations of strata.

Figure 14 is a diagrammatic cross section of a combination of marine and

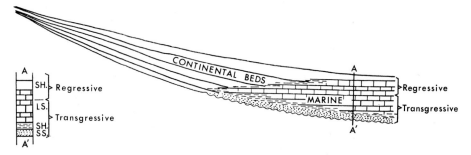

FIG. 14—Combination of transgressive and regressive marine sandstone, shale, and limestone overlain by regressive continental beds. Modified from Grabau (1913).

nonmarine sediments (Grabau, 1913, p. 742). The basal marine sandstone in the right half of the section is a transgressive unit. It is overlain by a thin veneer of marine shale, which is overlain by marine limestone. All three lithologic types were deposited in a sea that was transgressive until the shoreline reached the area at the middle of the figure. At that point, an uplift of the source area (on the left) caused abundant deposition of continental beds, both along the margins of the marine embayment and also seaward. Thus, the shoreline regressed in response to either the situation (1) where sediment supply exceeded the rate of subsidence, or (2) where an abundant supply of sediment was available under conditions of gradual uplift. Either regression was so rapid that it prevented sand sorting by wave action from forming a regressive sheet sandstone, or there was no available sand-size material marginal to the embayment to be reworked and sorted.

3

fundamental concepts related to sediments of marginal-marine area

PROFILES OF EQUILIBRIUM

In Figures 1–10, a sand-mud line is shown. It was pointed out that this line represents the maximum depth of wave agitation. It is also the depth above which marginal-marine sand is deposited and below which silts and clays accumulate. The intensity of wave energy varies greatly. Dunbar and Rodgers (1957, p. 130) stated that, "The depth of wave action falls almost to zero in calm weather and may rise to 300 feet or more during heavy storms. It varies from day to day with the passing storms, and from season to season as the prevailing weather changes. Currents generated by the winds likewise vary, and they commonly change direction with the shifting winds." Thus, the sand-mud line fluctuates in its vertical depth below the surface of the water. Lohse (1955, p. 99) pointed out that the surface wind is the principal agent controlling nontidal currents, surface waves, and the coastal-drifting processes in the northwest Gulf of Mexico. He made a distinction ". . . between prevailing winds, which blow most of the time, and predominant winds, which expend a greater amount of energy and usually do the greater amount of geologic work." The predominant winds, through the waves they generate, distribute the sediments and shape ". . . the bays, lagoons, barriers, passes, and sandsheet in southwest Texas."

Not all marginal-marine land surfaces have the same slope, nor are they always smooth. Under ideal conditions, sediment may be supplied at the shoreline in exactly the volume that can be kept in transit along the existing gradient. When this is the case, there is neither landward nor seaward transportation of rock debris, except for the silt- and clay-size materials held in suspension, and a profile of equilibrium is said to exist. Von Engeln and Caster (1952, p. 310) pointed out that a profile of equilibrium does not exist immediately after either uplift or subsidence of a coastal-plain area. The basinward slope may be either too gentle or too steep. If it is too gentle, waves and tides combine to scour and move bottom sediment in a landward direction, as shown in the lower half of Figure 15. Thus, the beach is extended in a seaward direction by deposition near and at the prograded shoreline. There is a regression of the shoreline which is unrelated either to rate of emergence or submergence, or to rate of sediment supply.

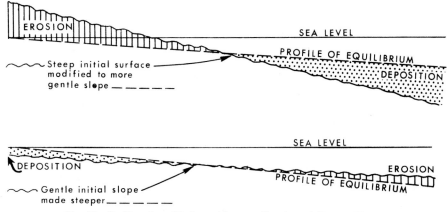

Fig. 15—Profiles of equilibrium. After von Engeln and Caster (1952).

If the basinward slope is too steep for a profile of equilibrium to exist, then the beach is eroded to form a wave-cut terrace, and the eroded materials are transported and deposited seaward, as shown in the upper half of Figure 15. Once an equilibrium condition is achieved in either of the situations illustrated in Figure 15, there is neither marked erosion nor deposition. An equilibrium condition is seldom maintained for any long period because of (1) great fluctuations in the amount of wave energy between storm and comparative calm and (2) seasonal variations in wind intensity. In fact, it is surprising that there is any orderliness or predictability with respect to the sediments that are deposited under such variable conditions.

GENETIC INCREMENT OF STRATA AND GENETIC SEQUENCE OF STRATA

From the preceding discussion it is evident that there are genetically related associations of sediment types in the marginal-marine environment. The writer recognizes two types of such associations (Busch, 1971). One is the *genetic increment of strata* (GIS) and the other is the *genetic sequence of strata* (GSS).

A GIS is defined as an interval of strata representing one cycle of sedimentation in which each lithologic component is related genetically to all others; the upper boundary must be a lithologic-time marker and the lower boundary may be either a lithologic-time marker, an unconformity, or a facies change from marine to nonmarine. It includes all sediments deposited during one stage of cyclic subsidence or cyclic uplift. It also may apply to one restricted sedimentary suite deposited during one stage of gradual subsidence or gradual uplift.

A GSS is defined as two or more contiguous genetic increments of strata representing more or less continuous sedimentation; angular unconformities cannot be present, but disconformities of limited extent may be present.

In both definitions the lithologic-time marker is critical because it represents contemporaneity of deposition. A thin bed of limestone, coal, bentonite, black shale, or siltstone may be a marker bed. Of the five, bentonite is considered to be the most reliable marker. The thickness of a shale sequence between two marker beds generally is fairly uniform within a local area. Marker beds generally diverge basinward on a regional scale. Abrupt changes in such intervals usually are due to facies changes, unconformities, or growth faulting, each of which must be clearly recognizable before utilizing the GIS and GSS concepts. In graphic illustration, the GIS is a particular case of a limited-interval isopach map, whereas the GSS is a special case of a gross-interval isopach map.

The basic concept and application of the GIS and GSS are not restricted to sandstone and shale; they also may be applied to carbonate-evaporite-shale sequences. Figure 16 diagrammatically illustrates three examples of GIS. The GIS shown in Figure 16A is defined at the top and bottom by beds of limestone. The base of the upper limestone and the top of the lower limestone could have been used instead of the reverse. The channel sand is not of the cut-and-fill type; the lower three fourths is the time equivalent of the laterally adjacent shale. This is an example of concurrent channel-sand and mud deposition. The practical value of the GIS shown in Figure 16A is that it reveals a systematic thickening basinward. Most channel sandstones trend in the same general direction as the thickening. The trends of the isopachs are approximately parallel with the paleodepositional strike of the strand. Channel sandstones generally are normal to this strike.

The paleogradient of the channel is determined by constructing an isopach map of the interval between the base of the sandstone and the upper (marker bed) limestone. These two datums diverge systematically and at approximately the same rate as the slope of the original stream valley.

The sandstone in Figure 16B is of different origin than that shown in Figure 16A. It is an offshore sandstone body trending nearly parallel with the shoreline. The upper limit of the GIS is a thin limestone bed, and the lower limit is a thin bentonite bed. An isopach map of this GIS shows systematic divergence or increase in the interval between these marker beds from left to right. Either an anomalous "terracing" effect or local thickening of the GIS takes place parallel with the isopachs. Such thickening is due to the relative noncompactibility of the sandstone of the bar as compared with the enclosing shale. The position and trend of this sandstone bar could be determined by mapping variations in thick-

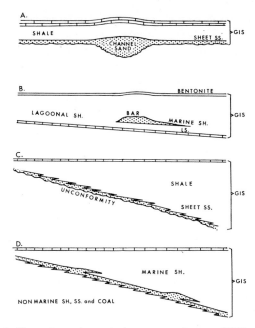

FIG. 16—Diagrammatic illustrations of genetic increments of strata (GIS). **A.** Channel and sheet sandstones with overlying shale and limestone; upper limit of GIS is defined by lithologic-time marker, base defined by unconformity. **B.** Sandstone bar bordered by lagoonal shale on one side and marine shale on other; upper and lower limits of GIS are defined by lithologic-time marker beds (bentonite and limestone). **C.** Sheet sandstone, resulting from cyclic subsidence, overlain by basinward-thickening marine shale; upper limit of GIS is defined by lithologic-time marker bed, base by unconformity. **D.** Sheet sandstone showing two areas of locally thicker sandstone at former stillstand positions of shoreline; upper boundary is defined by lithologic-time marker bed, base by facies change from continental to marine beds. After Busch (1971).

ness of the lagoonal and marine shales alone. Mapping of reciprocal thinning of the shale section above the thickest part of the sandstone is a valid method of tracing the sandstone body. The mapping of this shale interval is recommended in areas where most of the oil- or gas-producing wells were stopped short of the oil-water contact and, as a result, too few of the control points penetrate the entire thickness of the GIS.

Another idealized type of the GIS is shown in Figure 16C. A thick wedge of shale and a basal sheet of sandstone compose the GIS whose upper limit is a thin limestone bed and whose base is an unconformity. Isochrons are parallel with the thin limestone marker bed at the top and are crossed by the sheet sandstone. An isopach map of this GIS shows the approximate paleotopography of the unconformity at the base. This mapping technique is useful for tracing paleodepositional trends of beach sandstones where the individual sandstone beds are isolated and bear an *en échelon* relation to each other as a result of cyclic subsidence.

Figure 16D shows a GIS which is defined at the base by a facies change from marine to nonmarine strata. Neither an unconformity nor a time-lithologic marker bed is present at the base.

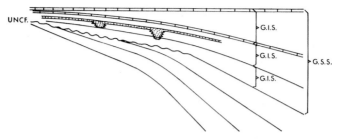

FIG. 17—Relation of genetic sequence of strata (GSS) to genetic increments of strata (GIS). After Busch (1971).

The relation of a GIS to a GSS is illustrated in Figure 17. The GSS, as shown here, includes three different types of GIS. The uppermost GIS is limited by thin limestone marker beds above and below and consists predominantly of shale. The middle GIS is similarly limited, but contains a sheet of sandstone which thickens downward into channel-like sandstone. The lowest GIS is limited by a marker bed at the top and by an unconformity at the base. Basinward (right), this unconformity disappears and a marker bed is present at the base of this GIS.

The principal value of the GSS concept is to reconstruct the paleodepositional configuration of a basin. Most sedimentary basins are so large that only a segment may be of interest. An isopach map of the GSS will reveal (1) basin shape, (2) paleodepositional trends, and (3) shelf, hinge line, and less stable basin areas. This type of isopach map can be constructed by use of widely scattered control points. Thus, it is of considerable value in preliminary studies and evaluations of stratigraphic sections and segments of sedimentary basins early in an exploration program. The GIS, however, is generally most applicable for detailed studies of individual sandstones. The significance of the shelf environment for the accumulation of reservoir-type sandstones is discussed by Weirich (1953).

The three lowest stratigraphic units shown on Figure 17 do not constitute a GIS individually, or a GSS collectively, in the area where they are defined at the top by the unconformity. Basinward from the unconformity, however, they may be considered as three GIS's and one GSS.

BEACH ENVIRONMENT

Several significant reservoir-type sandstones form in the beach environment. An understanding of them, however, must be predicated on background knowledge of modern beaches. The Beach Erosion Board of the U.S. Army Corps of Engineers has published some of the most meaningful studies of modern beaches. Figure 18 is a diagrammatic illustration of the major components of the beach environment. It is taken from Dunbar and Rodgers (1957, p. 68–70), who stated that,

The typical beach is divided into the relatively smooth sloping *foreshore*, which extends from lowest low water to a normally well-marked break in slope, called the *berm,* at about normal high water, and the rougher but relatively flat *backshore,* extending from the berm back to the farthest point reached by waves, which in natural conditions is commonly the base of a sea cliff or nip or the edge of a beach ridge or a line of sand dunes. Berms are mainly built during storms, and the bigger the storm the higher and more marked the berm; indeed, if a beach has experienced a series of storms of diminishing intensity, it may exhibit several berms, though the lower ones will be destroyed in the next great storm. The foreshore can commonly be further divided into the upper foreshore, which has a smooth profile, and the lower foreshore, which is broken by bars formed by the breakers at high stands of tide; similar bars may be present beyond low tide level, and the outer limit of the foreshore is not a line of major discontinuity. As with berms, the heaviest storms build the biggest bars and the farthest to sea, destroying all older bars; later weaker storms, or simply steady breakers of relatively constant size, can build smaller bars farther in, so that a given beach may have one bar one month and three or four another.

Except for the bars, the slope of the foreshore is a very shallow curve, slightly concave upward and flattening outward into the shelf profile. Its slope is governed by a number of factors; in general it is steeper if the material is coarse, if the shore is fully open to ocean waves, if the regimen of the sea includes heavy storms (and it is steeper right after heavy storms than after periods of ordinary weather), and perhaps also if the tidal range is high, provided tidal flats do not form. It does not appear to depend at all on the original slope of the terrain, and it is considerably steeper than the slope of most plains or continental shelves; hence if a shift in sealevel brings the shore onto such a plain or shelf, the waves gouge and build where they break until they have fashioned the proper beach profile, thus producing a barrier beach with an eroded zone in front and a lagoon or salt marsh behind. Relative to the rest of the over-all profile, this somewhat steeper part at the shore is called the *shore face.*

The material on such a beach is mostly or entirely sand. Finer materials are winnowed out by the waves and carried either into deep water or into protected bays and lagoons; gravel-size material, except for broken shells which are quickly worn down, is rarely available on low shores. At any one state of the waves, the size-sorting is apt to be excellent, each size having its appropriate station on the beach; but with alternating storm and calm, adjacent laminae commonly have rather different sizes, and the over-all sorting is only moderately good. Ordinarily the more resistant minerals, above all quartz, are concentrated on the beach, but there are many exceptions where non-resistant minerals are common or even

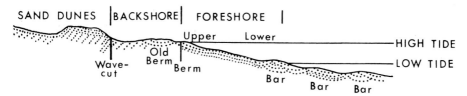

Fig. 18—Diagram of a beach and its component parts; vertically exaggerated. After Dunbar and Rodgers (1957), *Principles of Stratigraphy.* Copyright 1957 by John Wiley & Sons, Inc. Reprinted by permission of John Wiley & Sons, Inc.

dominant, as for instance where waves are relatively weak or have been at work only a short time or where quartz is uncommon or even lacking in the source area. Many Pacific islands have no quartz, and their beaches consist of calcite and aragonite grains, commonly fragments of shells and tests of foraminifera, of fragments of basalt, or of augite or olivine grains. Heavy resistant minerals, like ilmenite, magnetite, and zircon, are commonly sorted out from the quartz or other light minerals and concentrated in separated layers; on the Atlantic beaches of the southeastern United States, especially on older beaches now well above sealevel, commercial deposits of zircon and monazite have thus been formed. The coarser sand grains may be well rounded, but there seem to be as many exceptions as examples for this generalization. Shells may be present in abundance, and, of course, some beaches are made entirely of shell fragments, but on the whole potential fossils are relatively rare in the final deposits of normal quartz-sand beaches.

The stratification of beach deposits has been studied particularly by Thompson (1937) and by McKee (1953, p. 4–16). It differs markedly from one part of the beach to another. The upper foreshore has the most regular bedding, with long even laminae and cross-laminae exhibiting ordinarily only rather low-angle cross-stratification, commonly with a herringbone arrangement. The general dip is seaward at varying angles; the laminae may appear especially even and parallel in sections parallel to the shoreline, unless the beach is cusped. The lower foreshore with its bars is much more strongly cross-stratified, with cut-and-fill cross-bedding dipping both landward and seaward. The backshore is the most irregular; some beds show gentle even cross-stratification like that of the upper foreshore, but obvious cut-and-fill cross-bedding is also common, and patches of much disturbed sand and even lenses of silt or clay may be present. The dips of the cross-strata are irregular but most commonly are landward.

If material is being added to a beach by longshore currents or otherwise, the foreshore slope tends to remain nearly constant but the backshore widens as the beach advances seaward. As the landward parts of the backshore cease to be reached even by storm waves, beach ridges form parallel to the shore, marking the stages in the advance. If much material is available, as where streams contribute much sediment but the waves are strong enough to prevent delta formation, a wide belt of beach ridges may be formed; small ponds or swamps may be left between them. Almost invariably the wind becomes an important agent in these ridges, unless they are of gravel, and the belt behind the beach becomes a belt of sand dunes. If the supply of sand is large, the sand dunes may migrate inland and bury old lagoons, floodplain deposits, or whatever lies in their path.

The deposits of such sand dunes do not differ greatly from those of a desert except for their restriction to a belt just inland from a beach. The sand is normally considerably better size-sorted than on the beach and notably rounder, perhaps as much because round grains are selectively transported from the backshore by the wind as because of increased wear. Strong wedge-shaped cross-bedding is the rule. Lenses of silt and clay or even peat record lagoons or interridge lakes and swamps buried by the dunes.

modern examples
of beach sands

CHENIERS

General Characteristics

Cheniers were described first along the coast of southwest Louisiana by Russell and Howe in 1935. They later were described by Fisk (1955), Fisk and Mc-Farlan (1955), Byrne *et al.* (1959), and Gould and McFarlan (1959). Byrne *et al.* (1959, p. 2) described them as

> . . . long low ridges which rise above the marsh to form the only inhabitable areas on the plain. They range from a few inches to more than 10 feet in elevation, from 2 to 15 feet in thickness, and from 100 to 1500 feet in width; the average chenier is approximately 7 feet thick and about 600 feet wide. In several areas ridges converge to form composite cheniers which locally attain widths of 3000 feet. Individual cheniers extend coastwise for distances up to 30 miles without interruption. In cross section they are steep on the front and slope gently landward. In plan view they are generally slightly concave toward the gulf except near rivers or embayments where they are terminated and curve sharply landward. Washover deltas produce an irregular landward margin which contrasts noticeably with the smooth shoreward outline.

Their characteristic branching pattern and landward curve near stream mouths are illustrated in Figures 19 and 20. From these illustrations it is evident that the chenier plain of southwest Louisiana is as much as 10 mi (16 km) wide.

The base of an individual chenier deposit may be either flat or convex downward. The bottom commonly is downwarped a few feet below sea level as a

31

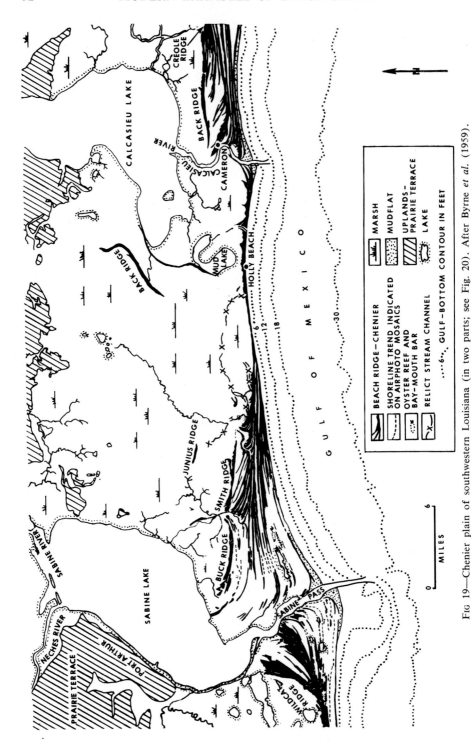

Fig 19—Chenier plain of southwestern Louisiana (in two parts; see Fig. 20). After Byrne *et al.* (1959).

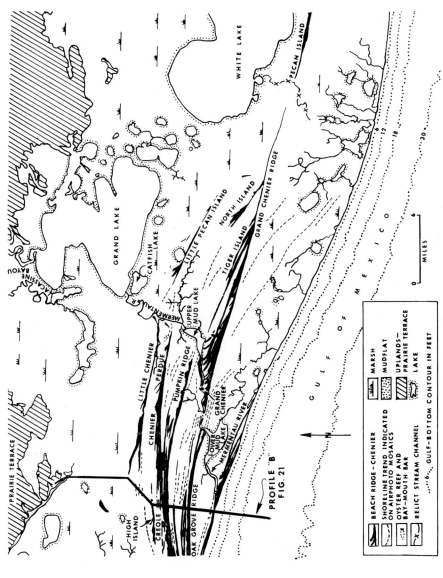

FIG. 20—Chenier plain of southwestern Louisiana (in two parts; see Fig. 19). After Byrne *et al.* (1959).

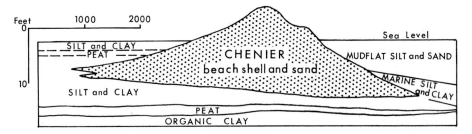

A. CROSS SECTION OF PECAN ISLAND CHENIER. VERTICAL EXAGGERATION, 200 X

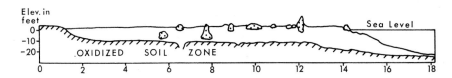

B.   PROFILE OF CHENIER PLAIN. VERTICAL EXAGGERATION, APPROX. 500X

FIG. 21—Cross sections of (A) Pecan Island chenier (right side of Fig. 20; after Gould and Morgan, 1962) and (B) chenier plain (Fig. 20; after Byrne *et al.*, 1959).

result of compaction of the underlying silts and clays. The cross-sectional shape of an individual chenier (Pecan Island) is illustrated in the upper half of Figure 21, which has a vertical exaggeration of 200 times. Some of the individual cheniers in the chenier plain, as illustrated in the lower half of Figure 21, are flat at the base, whereas others are convex. Collectively, they make up only a very small percentage of the total lithology of the chenier plain above the oxidized soil zone. Cheniers typically are present in multiples at approximately the same stratigraphic level; this characteristic is useful for subsurface identification.

Lithologically, cheniers consist principally of sand and shells with minor quantities of silt and clay. Byrne *et al.* (1959, p. 17) wrote that, "The shells, which make up 22 percent of the facies, occur as distinct layers up to several inches thick and as fragments disseminated throughout the sand."

Theory of Origin

Available information on cheniers indicates that the five following environmental conditions apparently are necessary to their development:

1. Low-lying marshy or swampy coastal plain adjacent to the delta of a river that transports a large load of sediment.

2. Longshore currents that transport delta (land-derived) sediments to the bordering coastal plain.

3. Periods of abundant supply of fine-grained sediment (to form mud flats) alternating with periods of slight sediment supply (during which beach ridges or cheniers are constructed).

4. Predominance of clay and silt with a minor amount of sand.

5. Moderate wave action along the shore.

Gould and Morgan (1962, p. 292) pointed out that,

> . . . alternations in coastal outbuilding and relative stability reflect pulsations in the supply of Mississippi River sediments carried into the area of longshore currents. Such pulsations have resulted not from changes in the load of the Mississippi but from wide lateral shifts in the position of the mouth during construction of the deltaic plain. Periods of rapid progradation resulted when the river discharged into the western part of the deltaic plain, whereas intervals of coastal stability and local retreat followed shifts in discharge to more easterly positions.

From the foregoing description of cheniers along the southwest Louisiana coast, it is apparent that this type of relic beach sand has considerable potential significance as a reservoir sandstone. Cheniers are genetically related to the deltaic environment. Additional sites where cheniers have been reported are in the vicinity of the Orinoco delta (Surinam and French Guiana) and adjacent to the deltas of the Amazon and San Francisco Rivers of Brazil. They are also thought to be present adjacent to the deltas of the Rhône (France) and Po (Italy) Rivers, as well as along the Gulf of Venezuela.

Although they rarely exceed 15 ft (4.6 m) in thickness along the southwest Louisiana coast, the cheniers may be much thicker, depending on such variables as the available supply of sand and shell material and the intensity of waves and longshore currents. Modern cheniers adjacent to the delta of the San Francisco River of northeastern Brazil have been reported (H. A. Chaves, Salvador, Brazil, personal commun., 1967) to be more than 40 ft thick. Similar thicknesses are postulated for some of their ancient counterparts.

Cheniers in the subsurface could be misinterpreted as offshore bars; both are deposited parallel with the shoreline, may be plano-convex in profile, and have fairly smooth seaward margins. As pointed out, however, cheniers generally are present in multiples at the same stratigraphic position. Also, in comparison to offshore bars, they generally are narrower in plan view and thin more abruptly basinward. Cheniers are deposited *at* the shoreline, whereas offshore bars generally are deposited some distance offshore and are separated from the mainland by a lagoon.

Most petroleum exploration geologists have not been looking for cheniers in

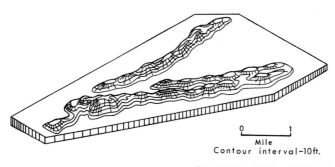

0 ____ 1
Mile
Contour interval—10ft.

CHANUTE POOL, KANSAS

FIG. 22—Possible example of a chenier. After Dillard *et al.* (1941).

the subsurface because information about this type of sandstone body has not been available until recently. None of the standard textbooks on petroleum geology make any reference to cheniers as either real or potential sites of stratigraphic oil and gas accumulation. Fisk (1955) and Byrne *et al.* (1959) noted the similarity of chenier sands to certain subsurface lenticular sandstones. They referred to the Chanute pool (Fig. 22) of southeastern Kansas (Dillard *et al.,* 1941) as a possible example of an ancient chenier-type reservoir. The sandstone body of this pool exceeds 40 ft (12 m) in thickness and diverges in a manner similar to that of modern cheniers.

OFFSHORE BARS

General Characteristics

Offshore bars, called "longshore bars" and "barrier islands" by some, are elongate islands of sand deposited parallel with the shore of the mainland and separated from it by lagoons which commonly are marshy. If these elongate sand bodies are attached to a bulge of the mainland and extend nearly across a neighboring bay, they are called "baymouth bars."

Systems of offshore bars are particularly well developed along the Atlantic and Gulf Coasts of North America and along the south shore of the North Sea in Europe. They generally are interrupted by tidal inlets and have a smooth seaward margin and an irregular lagoonal margin. In areas of considerable tidal range the lagoonal side of an offshore bar may be comparatively straight as a result of rather pronounced flood- and ebb-tidal scouring. Longshore currents commonly occur on the seaward side of offshore bars, tending to keep this side of the sand body straight and to lengthen the bar.

Bernard *et al.* (1962, p. 185) described "the characteristic topographic features of barrier islands" as being

> . . . low, parallel, occasionally recurved beach ridges, spits, shallow swales between beach ridges, sand dunes of various types, active and abandoned tidal channels, tidal deltas, and wash-over fans. . . . The bay side of most barrier islands is characterized by a large number of abandoned tidal channels or "guts" which trend approximately at right angles to the long axis of the island. Many "guts" are former swale areas between hooked spit accretions formed at the ends of the islands. Tidal processes and storm-generated wash-over currents keep most "guts" open. The sediments forming these islands consist principally of fine to very fine, well sorted sand and shell fragments.

Elongate beach ridges extend along the subaerially exposed part of an offshore bar and have a gentle landward slope and a steeper seaward slope. The maximum height of such ridges along the Gulf Coast, where they are locally modified by wind activity to form hummocky sand dunes, is approximately 12 ft (3.6 m).

Tidal channels, deltas, and washover fans are characteristically associated with offshore bars. Bernard *et al.* (1962, p. 187) pointed out that:

> Tidal deltas occur both on the seaward and bayward side of tidal passes crossing or separating barrier islands, bars, giant ripples, sand flats and marshes. Shoals

caused by tidal deltas on the seaward side of the tidal passes are indicated by the position of the breakers, which occur some distance offshore. Tidal deltas on the bayward side of tidal passes also produce shoals, but are seldom indicated by breakers in the more protected bays.

Following the closure of tidal passes on the Gulf side by the deposition of beach, shoreface, and channel sand, the "delta" on the seaward side is destroyed by subsequent marine erosion, but the tidal delta in the bay may continue to grow periodically by the deposition of sediment transported by storm wash-over currents which temporarily reopen the tidal passes. At this stage of development much of the area of the "delta" is emergent and is called a wash-over fan.

Theories of Origin

Theories of origin of offshore bars, or barrier islands, are varied and numerous. In 1845, Élie de Beaumont postulated that offshore bars are formed by waves which erode material from the ocean bottom and deposit it when it no longer can be carried. Gilbert (1885) reported that offshore bars are solely the result of transportation and deposition by longshore currents. D. Johnson (1919) related all offshore bars to the youthful stages of emergent coastlines. He attributed initial deposition to two opposing forces of energy, namely, waves and undertow. Where waves drag the bottom, their energy is partly dissipated and offset a little farther landward by the opposing energy of the undertow. As the submarine bar grows vertically by accretion, longshore currents, resulting from waves that strike the shore at an oblique angle, cause extension of the bar in a direction parallel with the shoreline. He believed that further growth of a bar is due to a lowering of sea level. Evans (1942) believed that offshore bars are a result of an equilibrium condition of wave energy and that neither emergence nor submergence of the coastline is of any great significance. Shepard (1950a) wrote:

> Plunging breakers excavate the bottom, producing longshore troughs. The material thus set into suspension is moved parallel to the shore by currents which turn seaward into rip channels forming gaps in the longshore-bars. Some of the bars and troughs are exposed by low tide. The sand carried outside the bar is spread out over the slope by the expanding head of the rip current. Thence the shoreward drag under wave crests carries it back to build up the longshore-bars outside the troughs. The growth of these bars is limited by the depth at which waves will plunge and prevent further sand encroachment.

It is well established that severe storms and hurricanes are capable of completely destroying many well-developed submerged bars. Zenkovich (1962) suggested that bars may be formed along a submerging coast as well as along an emerging coast. He listed two essential conditions for offshore-bar development along a submergent coast—the existence of a ridge on the shore and the existence of an underwater slope which is steeper than the general slope of the land behind the ridge. This rise is presumably the berm which, when sea level rises, moves in a landward direction as the waves pass over its crest. Concurrently, it becomes higher as sediment is deposited on it. This process continues as long as there is a slow rise in sea level. Guilcher (1958, p. 88, 90) also recognized that offshore bars are developed along submerging as well as emerging shorelines. He believed that offshore bars usually are driven shoreward but that one or more narrow channels remain open if the sand body tends to block a sizable stream.

A series of interesting and instructive laboratory experiments was performed by McKee and Sterret (1961) in an effort to learn more about the form and structure of longshore bars and beaches. Their experiments were conducted in a 46-ft (14 m) wave tank. It was noted that major differences in primary structure and shape of a sand body can be effected by changing each of these variables: slope of the sand floor, intensity of wave action, and supply of sand. McKee and Sterret (1961, p. 13) noted that:

> Longshore bars are produced at the point of wave break. In very shallow water an emergent bar commonly forms; in somewhat deeper water a submarine bar is built; and in still deeper water no bar forms. Increase in intensity of waves tends to build a bar toward, and even onto, the beach. Weaker waves build bars upward to form barriers, with lagoons to shoreward. Abundant sand furnished on the seaward side of a growing bar simulates conditions caused by longshore and rip currents, and causes gentle seaward-dipping beds to form. In contrast, a limited sand supply results in growth of bars that characteristically have shoreward-dipping strata of steeper angle.
>
> Beach strata normally dip seaward at low angles from the crest to a point below water level. Offshore, the seaward extensions of these gently dipping beds include fore-set beds with relatively high angles which form a shoreface terrace. The sand body comprised of both sets of bedding builds outward if a large supply of sand is furnished. In shallow water, however, or at moderate depth where waves are strong, the period of beach growth is limited by the deposition of longshore bars which eliminate wave action as they grow into barriers and form lagoons. Under conditions in which no bar is built, growth of the beach and shoreface terrace is controlled by the amount of sand available; the proportion of top-set to fore-set beds is determined by the strength of waves.

It is apparent that there is no unanimity of opinion regarding the origin of offshore bars. It is clear, however, that longshore currents and waves are the energy forces operative in their formation. Furthermore, they form under conditions of emergence or submergence, or stillstand of a shoreline. Variables such as differences in depositional slope, intensity of wave energy, and supply of sand all have a direct bearing on both the internal structure and the shape of the sand body. It probably is because of these variables that it is difficult to generalize about the origin of offshore bars in different areas.

Perhaps the best way to understand offshore bars is to review the characteristics of a few modern bars and then review their subsurface analogues.

Middle Sound Area, Onslow Bay, North Carolina

The Middle Sound area of Onslow Bay was studied by Miller (1962), who presented an offshore-bar–forming situation which appears to have considerable application in the subsurface. The Atlantic coastal plain in this area, according to Miller, is a structurally stable depositional surface in which the shoreline is regressing as a result of deposition. Blanton (1963), however, disagreed regarding the stability of the depositional surface. He presented convincing evidence that the Middle Sound bars have persisted through as much as 15 ft (4.6 m) of subsidence. Blanton (p. 95) wrote, "This creates a paradox of regressive sediments in a transgressive sea." The Middle Sound is an area of a 30-in. (76 cm) diurnal tide and a northeasterly flowing longshore current. A barrier bar parallels the shoreline and consists of a series of narrow, elongate islands with an average width of 1,050 ft (320 m) and a maximum height of 35–40 ft (11–12 m) above sea level (Fig. 23). Miller (1962, p. 234, 235) pointed out that,

> With the exception of the strand-line deposits the sediments are extensively cross bedded in typical eolian fashion, well defined by the laminae of dark-colored heavy minerals. . . . The steepest relief along the bar (from sediment surface to sediment surface) is on the shoreward side where it is backed up by a lagoonal channel. The seaward side of the bar slopes irregularly toward the beach through a series of low relief terraces. The thirty-inch tide has developed a beach approximately one hundred yards wide that is made up wholly of clean, fine and medium grained sand, shells, and shell fragments. With only minor exceptions, the dip (source direction) of the individual sand lentils of the beach is toward the sea. Localized drainage "guts" in the littoral zone create a gentle hill and valley relationship, with one or two feet of relief, at right angles to the shoreline. . . .
>
> The inlet channels that separate the individual islands of the barrier bar are 500 to 1000 feet wide and have a hard clay-packed substratum 10 to 15 feet below mean sea level. There is little chance for detritus to be deposited in the inlet because of the nearly continuous currents that sweep through the opening during the flood and ebb of the tides. During flood tides, the surface water moves through the inlet at 10 to 15 miles per hour (visual examination). Sand has accumulated in a deltaic pattern on both the marine and lagoon sides of the inlets in conjunction with this diminishing current flow.

Miller (1962) pointed out that the sands of the barrier bars thin and slope gradually in a seaward direction. The seaward gradient of the depositional surface ranges from 20 to 25 ft/mi (3.8–4.7 m/km) for a distance of 1.0–1.5 mi (1.6–2.4 km), which coincides with a water depth of approximately 40 ft (12 m). Beyond the 40-ft (12 m) depth the sand consists of a thin veneer (measured in inches) lying on a hard, clayey base. The sand veneer has an average gradient of 2–3 ft/mi (0.38–0.57 m/km) and extends many miles out to sea to water depths of 50–60 ft (15–18 m). Miller postulated that this veneer, or apron, of sand is in transit and ultimately will be deposited in water depths of less than 40 ft (12 m). He made special note (p. 239) of ". . . the reoccurrence of the 40 foot thickness (and depth) value which seems to be a critical height (see Bernard *et al.,* 1961, and LeBlanc *et al.,* 1961) as well as a critical depth for shore line and bar deposits just as it has been throughout geologic time."

The dimensions of the depositional features of Middle Sound are illustrated in Figure 24. From this figure it is apparent that the width of the lagoon ranges

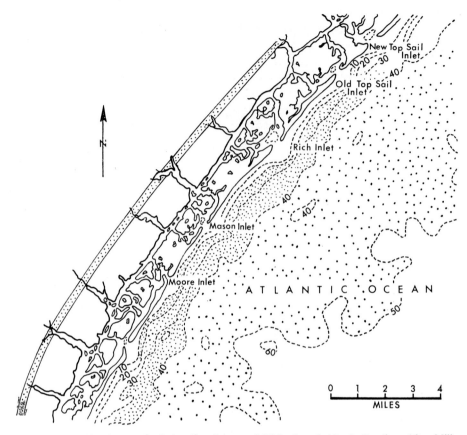

Fig. 23—Depositional pattern of shoreline features, Middle Sound, North Carolina. After Miller (1962).

from 1.1 to 1.7 mi (1.8–2.7 km). Except for the lagoonal channels, it consists principally of intertidal mud flats and low, flat-topped, heavily vegetated islands. The islands consist of oyster reefs covered with a thin veneer of black mud. Marsh grasses and reeds grow in this mud. The principal sediment of the lagoon is a black organic mud. Thin, discontinuous patches of sand are present along the sides of the distributary channels.

Miller (1962) postulated that the position and width of the part of the offshore bar above sea level are established and controlled by the profile of equilibrium. He wrote (p. 241):

> . . . in general (and within limits), the steeper the submarine gradient, the narrower the bar. If the gradient becomes too steep, no bar is developed because the sediments are distributed laterally. If the gradient becomes too shallow, the bar reverts to a broad flat beach that accretes seaward. . . . The profile in turn is established in response to the amount and type of detritus available and the ability of the currents and wave action to transport the detritus. . . . hurricanes and other violent disturbances . . . alter the pattern periodically, but for the most part, the principal

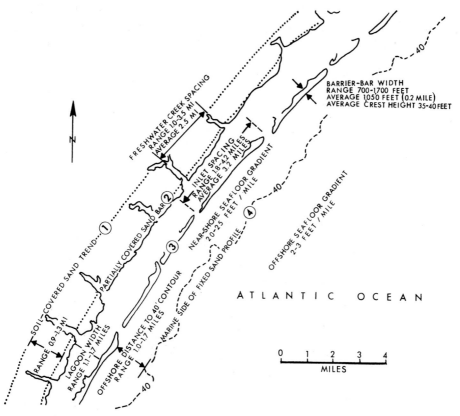

FIG. 24—Dimensions of depositional features shown in Figure 23, Middle Sound, North Carolina. After Miller (1962).

direction of current movement is from the deltas to the sea and then from the sea to the barrier bar. From a practical standpoint, the beginning and the end of each significant depositional pattern is directly related to changes in position of sea level with respect to river deltas.

The positions and trends of two soil-covered ridges on the shore can be seen in Figures 23 and 24. Miller considers these ridges to represent earlier stages of barrier-bar development. He infers that the barrier bar at Middle Sound represents

> . . . a single stage in an overall cyclic process of "shore line jump" in which each new mature bar-lagoon complex will add 1.5 miles (or progressively less near the deltas) of new shore to the coastal plain. In other words, the present barrier bar was preceded by similar[ly] trending bars in the past and will be succeeded by more barrier bars in the future. . . .

Figures 25 and 26 are his diagrammatic attempts to explain the stage development of a regressive barrier-bar sequence. In Figure 26 the plus signs over the deltas indicate an excess supply of sediment. The middle part of the em-

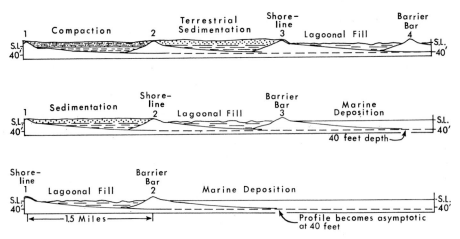

Fig. 25—Diagrammatic cross sections, showing stage development of regressive barrier-bar sequence. After Miller (1962).

bayment has not yet reached equilibrium and, therefore, is designated with a minus sign. When equilibrium ultimately is reached in the middle of the embayment, ". . . a new and younger bar will begin to form at the delta and the process will be repeated as shown."

Miller was well aware that his multiple-bar hypothesis does not necessarily apply along all shorelines because of the numerous variables involved in the establishment of an equilibrium condition. He did, however, use the Middle Sound situation of the North Carolina coast as a means of explaining the multiple bars comprising the Fall River sandstone along the east side of the Powder

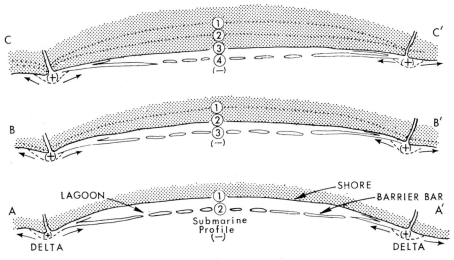

Fig. 26—Diagrammatic plan view of stage development of regressive shorelines. After Miller (1962).

River basin of northeastern Wyoming (Miller, 1962). The writer believes that Miller's explanation for multiple lenses of marginal-marine sands has considerable application in subsurface stratigraphic analysis. A case in point is the Tonkawa sandstone (Pennsylvanian) of northwestern Oklahoma. It consists of several lenticular sandstone bodies which were deposited parallel with the ancient shoreline and which bear a vertical *en échelon* relation to each other. The sandstone lenses are separated by thin shale "breaks." A multiple regressive-bar arrangement can readily be interpreted from detailed electric-log profiles and offers the only logical explanation for the presence of water in wells updip from wells producing hydrocarbons.

Galveston Barrier Island

Galveston Island, off the Texas Gulf Coast, is an excellent example of an offshore bar. Abandoned beach ridges and intervening low swales, which are well preserved in the central part of the island, clearly demonstrate the seaward growth of the island by continued addition of sand by longshore currents (Fig. 27). It grew southwestward by beach-spit, tidal-channel, and tidal-delta accretion in the direction of longshore-current transport. Radiocarbon dating of shell beds within the sand body clearly indicates seaward accretionary growth of this barrier island. Sea level reached its present position a little over 3,500 years ago when Galveston Island was a small bar situated about 4 mi (6.4 km) offshore on the southwest side of the mouth of Galveston Bay. The combined efforts of winds, surface currents, and waves refracting shoreward produced the westerly longshore currents necessary to add material to this bar, which grew into a barrier island. Most of the sand was derived from an easterly source, whereas much of the silt and clay probably were contributed by the Trinity and San Jacinto Rivers. Bernard *et al.* (1962, p. 196) pointed out that the depositional features ". . . consist principally of numerous narrow, parallel beach ridges which vary

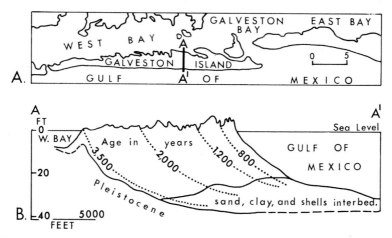

FIG. 27—**A.** Galveston Island, Texas Gulf Coast. **B.** Profile *A-A'*, Galveston Island, showing radiocarbon dates of shell beds. After Bernard *et al.* (1962).

in elevation from a few inches to twelve feet, and intervening swales. These features trend almost parallel to the present shoreline, but are recurved along the backside and younger western ends of the islands." Four breaker bars normally can be seen from the beach. Their positions and height, and the number visible, vary with wave height and direction, tides, and possibly longshore currents. Depending on prevailing conditions, these bars may move up the upper part of the shoreline and beach, transporting sand to the upper shoreface and beach environments.

The surface sands of Galveston Island are very well sorted, fine to very fine grained. Sand containing shells extends gulfward to the 30-ft (9 m) subaqueous contour; seaward from this the bottom consists of silt and clay with shells. Sedimentary structures are useful in distinguishing most of the Holocene facies of the barrier island. Most of the bay deposits are burrowed and churned by organisms. Bedding and laminations are common in the sand and clay in the tidal-delta and bay deposits near channels, where the sediments frequently are reworked and deposited by currents. Lamination and very low-angle cross-laminae are the most common structures in the sand deposited in the upper foreshore of the beach environment. The middle-shoreface deposits consist of markedly burrowed, churned, laminated, bedded, and in places crossbedded shelly-sand and shell layers. Elongate sand grains in the beach deposits are preferentially aligned at right angles to the long dimensions of the barrier island. This orientation is parallel with the direction of motion of the last waves to act upon the grains of sand.

Ojo de Liebre, Baja California, Mexico

It generally is thought that offshore bars are separated from the mainland by marshy lagoons containing comparatively stagnant water. In a study made by Phleger and Ewing (1962) in the Ojo de Liebre area of Baja California, it is clearly pointed out that a lagoon behind an offshore bar may be a high-energy environment in which the dominant sediment deposited is sand. The submarine topography of the lagoon behind the offshore bar is illustrated in Figure 28. There are numerous deep tidal channels fanning out landward; they are bordered by large intertidal flats. The walls of these channels are quite steep. Deep channels are present on both sides of the inlet directly behind the lagoon barrier. The upper surface of the offshore bar has numerous high barchan dunes. The leeward faces of some of these dunes merge directly with the edges of the two major lagoonal channels. The depth of the tidal inlet ranges from 20 to 48 ft (6.0–14.6 m). The north major channel behind the bar is 40–50 ft (12.2–15.2 m) deep, and the channel south of the inlet is approximately 40 ft (12.2 m) deep. These deeply scoured channels are attributed chiefly to a maximum tidal current of 2.5 knots which, in turn, is the result of a tidal range of 4–9 ft (1.2–2.7 m). The water of the channels is quite turbulent.

A narrow strip of land connecting the offshore bar with the mainland separates an originally larger lagoon into two parts. The northern lagoon is Laguna Guerrero Negro and the southern one is Laguna Ojo de Liebre. This lagoon "divider" consists of sand which was deposited where the flood tides, sweeping through the two tidal inlets, moved in opposite directions behind the offshore bar.

Phleger and Ewing (1962, p. 145) wrote that,

Most sediment is fine to very fine well sorted and slightly skewed sand. The immediate source of the sand is the lagoon barrier, open ocean beach, and near shore

FIG. 28—Offshore bars and lagoons, Ojo de Liebre, Baja California, Mexico. After Phleger and Ewing (1962).

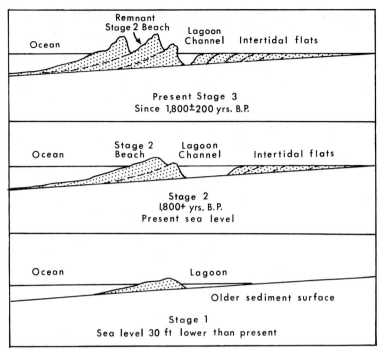

FIG. 29—Stages of offshore-bar and lagoon development, Ojo de Liebre, Baja California, Mexico. After Phleger and Ewing (1962).

zone. . . . The average sand is approximately 95 per cent quartz, 4 per cent dark minerals, and 1 per cent or less Foraminifera and shell. . . . Processes of sedimentation include wind delivery of sand from the barrier and distribution by turbulent tidal currents. Most deposition occurs on intertidal flats and in the inner lagoon, due to loss of water turbulence. The channels next to the barrier tend to maintain themselves.

In explaining the offshore bar at Ojo de Liebre, Phleger and Ewing considered three conditions to be essential. They are (1) abundant supply of sand, (2) gently sloping foundation, and (3) wave action along an exposed coast. Most of the sand is distributed along the coast by longshore drift. Three stages are exhibited in Figure 29, showing the development of this offshore bar. It is believed to have begun as a fringing beach on a gently sloping coastal plain at a time when sea level was 40 ft (12.2 m) lower than at present. In Stage 1, sea level is shown at a position 30 ft (9.1 m) lower than at present. Phleger and Ewing (1962, p. 174–175) stated that,

This depth is based on the presence of older sediment at about −40 feet in the inlets to lagunas Ojo de Liebre and Guerrero Negro. . . . This older sediment is believed to be the foundation on which the present barrier was deposited. Sea level must have remained at 40 feet below the modern level long enough to establish an extensive beach. . . .

When the beach sand was above high tide, wind action began the formation of dunes, and the barrier grew upward. With the slow rise of sea level the barrier built

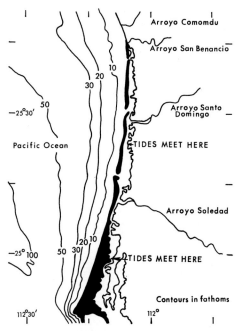

FIG. 30—Laguna Santo Domingo, Baja California, Mexico. After Phleger and Ewing (1962).

up in the same location since a ridgelike foundation had been established against which sand could be piled. At Stage 2 . . . the sea was at its present level. A deposit of beach molluscs is found in the barrier approximately 1 mile inland from the present beach. . . . The material in this beach has been dated by radiocarbon as 1800 ± 200 years B.P. At this time the barrier was 1 mile narrower than at present. Stage 3 is a diagrammatic representation of the present barrier.

Laguna Santo Domingo, Baja California, Mexico

An extensive barrier beach is located approximately 200 mi (320 km) south of Ojo de Liebre in an area known as Laguna Santo Domingo (Fig. 30). This offshore-bar complex averages 0.5 mi (0.8 km) in width except near the southern end, where it is much wider. Barchans ranging from 40 to 50 ft (12.2–15.2 m) high are present on the upper surface. The bar is bordered by relatively deep channels on the west side of the lagoon. The lagoon ranges from 0.5 to 2 mi (0.8–3.2 km) in width and, except for the deep channels, consists of tidal flats and marsh areas, bordered by mangrove. Phleger and Ewing (1962, p. 169) reported that, "At most stations the sediment is fine sand with good sorting and little skewness. . . . All samples contain significant quantities of apatite. An analysis of the lagoon barrier sand made by a mining company revealed an average of approximately 4 per cent apatite in the upper 20–40 feet of sediment." This barrier beach appears to be in an earlier stage of development than that of Ojo de Liebre. The absence of "divider" ridges of sand at the several positions where flood tides meet behind the barrier (see Fig. 30) is evidence for this observation.

5

ancient examples
of beach sandstones

"SECOND BEREA" SANDSTONE, APPALACHIAN BASIN

An excellent subsurface example of an offshore bar is present in southeastern Ohio, extending from Gallia County north to Muskingum County (Fig. 31). This bar is composed of "Second Berea" sandstone, which is Early Mississippian. This offshore bar fringes the southeastern part of a large, south-trending deltaic wedge of redbeds (Bedford), which also are Early Mississippian. Both this delta and the "Second Berea" sandstone are described and illustrated by Pepper *et al.* (1954) in a classic paper. The remarkable part of this study is that it was based almost entirely on drillers' logs and outcrop data because almost no electric-log data were available for this area at the time of the investigation. They used more than 1,300 drillers' logs in outlining the shape, contouring the variations in thickness, and plotting cross sections of this offshore bar. They (Pepper *et al.,* 1954, p. 56) described the "Second Berea sand" as

> . . . an ancient shoreline deposit strongly resembling a modern barrier bar, such as those along the Gulf Coast of Texas. The sand body is about 185 miles long, 3 to 15 miles wide. The relatively straight eastern margin is the seaward side of the offshore bar, and the irregular western margin is the result of unequal deposition in the lagoon on the landward side of the bar.

Over much of the area of its development, the "Second Berea" offshore bar is less than 20 ft (6.1 m) thick but locally exceeds 30 ft (9.1 m). The base is flat and the upper surface is convex. The sandstone thins more abruptly eastward from the crest than it does to the west, toward the lagoon. This sandstone body is attached to the mainland at its north end (Fig. 31). One of the distributary

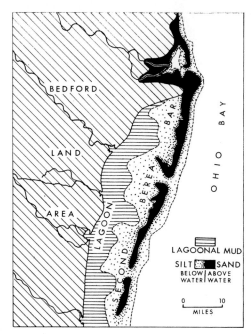

Fig. 31—"Second Berea" bar during time of Bedford deposition. After Pepper *et al.* (1944).

systems of the Bedford delta discharged its sediment in this area. To the north of this area of discharge a south-trending spit approximates a baymouth bar in that it isolates a restricted lagoon environment. A tidal inlet is conspicuous in the central part of the offshore bar. On either side of this inlet the sandstone of the bar bends abruptly back into the lagoon. A tidal delta with diverging fingers presumably fanned out into the lagoon.

The thicker parts of this offshore bar have produced considerable quantities of gas and a minor amount of oil. Pepper *et al.* (1944) pointed out that,

> Production of natural gas in the Second Berea is controlled both by the thickness of the sand body and by the grain size of the sand. Normally, the best gas wells occur in the thicker sand. However, in the thick sand east of the crest of the bar a high percentage of wells have been dry, probably because the grain size is small and because the sand contains a high percentage of silt. On the west or lagoon side of the crest, however, production is sometimes obtained in as little as 10 feet of sand, but seldom in less than 10 feet. Northwest of Morgan Township, Morgan County, in the area described as a bay enclosed by a spit and along the northward extension of the old mainland shore, the sand is rarely productive.

In this bay the sand is exceptionally silty and very low in permeability.

SABER BAR, DENVER-JULESBURG BASIN, COLORADO

Griffith (1966) presented an interesting and instructive analysis of the Saber bar, which is developed in the Upper Cretaceous "D" sandstone on the west-

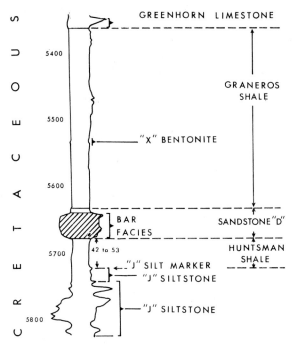

Fɪɢ. 32—Typical electric log in Saber field, Colorado. After Griffith (1966).

ward-sloping east flank of the Denver-Julesburg basin. The mapped part of this feature is about 10 mi (16.0 km) long and approximately 1 mi (1.6 km) wide. The maximum thickness is about 45 ft (13.7 m). The only oil-productive parts of this offshore bar are where west-plunging structural noses cross its depositional trend. The base ranges from 42 to 55 ft (12.8–16.8 m) above the "J" siltstone marker, and the interval between is called the Huntsman shale (Fig. 32). This fairly uniform thickness of shale above a lithologic reference datum indicates that the base of the overlying offshore bar was essentially flat at the time of deposition. Griffith (1966, p. 2115) stated that, "A subsurface structural map was made on a datum described as the base of the sandstone bar or its correlative away from the bar," and that the illustration (Fig. 33A) ". . . shows the topography of the sea floor on which the bar was deposited." The essentially flat base of an offshore bar is controlled by wave base, and if Figure 33A represents topography on the seafloor, the sandstone body should be roughly parallel with the sinuous trends of the structural contours of this figure. Rather than representing topography, however, Figure 33A actually represents the present structure of the base of the Saber bar; this structure was superimposed in post-Cretaceous time. Griffith (1966, p. 2116) further stated, "The base of the sea floor on which the bar was deposited appears to be a relatively smooth, gently sloping surface," an observation with which the writer agrees completely.

The Saber bar is one of the very few examples of subsurface offshore bars for which permeability studies of cores have been used to identify and correlate internal structural features, as shown in Figure 34. Griffith (1966, p. 2117) stated,

> Within the Saber bar, the presence of several layers can be inferred by correlating intervals of similar permeability between wells (all of which were cored). The bar graphs next to each of the five wells on the cross section illustrate both the vertical and horizontal changes in permeability that occur. Permeability generally increases toward the upper surface and the seaward side of the bar. Whereas lateral changes are gradational, vertical changes are abrupt and emphasize the marked difference in energy levels at the time of deposition of various layers.

BISTI BAR, SAN JUAN BASIN

The Bisti field, of the San Juan basin of New Mexico, is undoubtedly the best-documented example of an ancient offshore bar that appears in the literature. This field actually consists of a series of three closely related offshore bars, which Sabins (1963) referred to as the "Bisti bar complex." The oil field itself is approximately 3 mi (4.8 km) wide and more than 30 mi (48.3 km) long. Estimated recoverable primary reserves are 1,100 bbl/acre, and estimated secondary reserves are 900 bbl/acre. Accumulation is strictly stratigraphic; the strata have a regional northeastward homoclinal dip of approximately 75 ft/mi (14.2 m/km).

Sabins (1963, p. 194, 195) pointed out that,

> The Bisti stratigraphic trap is a sand bar complex developed during one of the regressive and transgressive sedimentary cycles that characterized Late Cretaceous sedimentation of the San Juan basin. Throughout most of Late Cretaceous time the San Juan basin was a marginal embayment of the sea that covered the Western

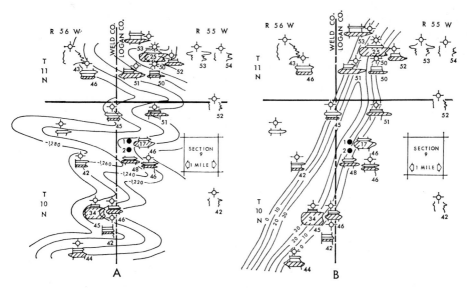

FIG. 33—**A.** Structural contour map of base of Saber bar; contours in feet. **B.** Isopach map of Saber bar; contours in feet. After Griffith (1966).

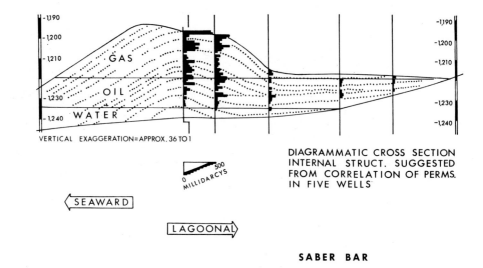

FIG. 34—West-east cross section across Saber bar (above) showing internal structure and external shape. Compare with bar produced in laboratory (below) by McKee and Sterret (1961). After Griffith (1966).

Interior. It was not until the end of Cretaceous time that the San Juan structural basin formed as a result of marginal tectonic uplifts.

The trap itself is made up of three individual offshore bars, which Sabins designated as the Marye, Huerfano, and Carson sandstones. The principal producing member is the Marye sandstone, which ranges from 1 to 2 mi (1.6–3.2 km) in width, has a maximum thickness of 40 ft (12.2 m), and is more than 30 mi (48.3 km) long. The Huerfano sandstone member underlies the Marye sandstone and is separated from it by a thin shale (Fig. 35). It is limited to the southeastern part of the pool area, as shown in Figure 36. It is less than 30 ft (9.1 m) thick, approximately 2 mi (3.2 km) wide, and about 24 mi (38.6 km) long. The Carson sandstone is present only in the central part of the Bisti field. It is less than 30 ft (9.1 m) thick and less than 1 mi (1.6 km.) wide, and has a known length of 9 mi (14.5 km). It is situated southwest of, and trends parallel with, the Huerfano bar, and the two bars are at the same stratigraphic position relative to the underlying main Gallup Sandstone. An isopach map of all bar sandstones of the Bisti field is shown in Figure 37.

Sabins' study is of particular value in subsurface studies of offshore bars because he presents core thin-section criteria for distinguishing bar facies, forebar, backbar, and beach sand facies. These thin-section criteria, which include texture, mineralogy, and paleontology, are summarized in Table 3; the reader is referred to Sabins (1963) for more detailed tables of criteria.

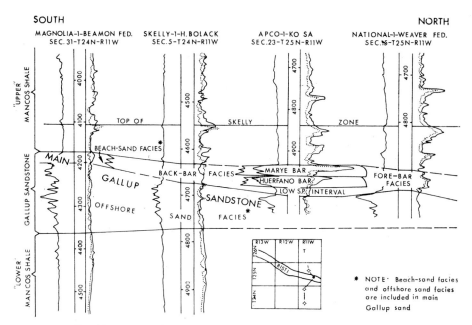

FIG. 35—Stratigraphic nomenclature in Bisti field. After Sabins (1963).

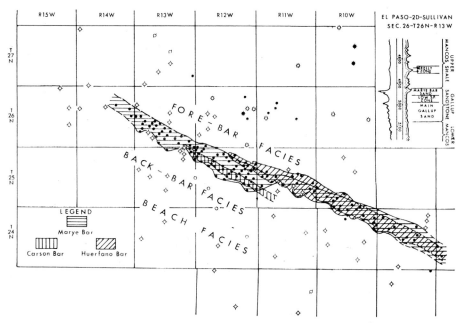

FIG. 36—Outlines of effective bar sandstones. From microlog interpretations by G. M. Nevers (Sabins, 1963).

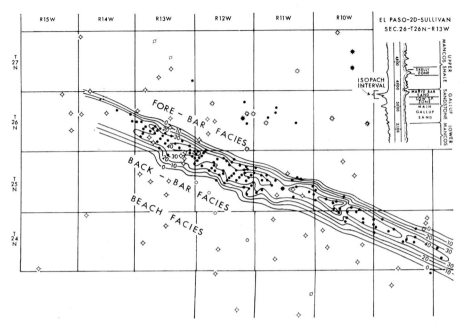

FIG. 37—Isopach map of all bar sandstones of Bisti field, based on self-potential curve of electric logs. Isopach interval, 10 ft. After Sabins (1963).

In summarizing his observations regarding the Bisti bar complex, Sabins (1963, p. 227, 228) stated,

These petrographic characteristics constitute criteria for recognizing the individual facies. This makes it possible to discriminate facies that have identical megascopic and electric log characteristics. For example, at Bisti the high glauconite content of Bar sands distinguishes them from the similar appearing Beach sand facies which lacks glauconite. The open marine assemblage of *Inoceramus,* collophane, and calcite-filled planktonic Foraminifera in the Fore-Bar facies distinguishes it from the Back-Bar facies which contains a restricted marine fauna of pyrite-filled benthonic Foraminifera.

Vertical gradients of sandstone texture and primary dolomite grain distribution are valuable for reconstructing the depositional history. These gradients, plus paleotopographic mapping show that the Gallup sedimentary cycle in the Bisti area began with regressive deposition of the Off-shore sand facies. Northwest-trending longshore bar and trough topography was formed on the upper surface of the Off-shore sand unit. A pulse of subsidence and possibly a minor disconformity account for the sharp contact between the Off-shore sand facies and the overlying Low SP facies. Wave action concentrated at a seaward-facing break in slope then winnowed the clay and concentrated the sand of the Low SP facies to form the Bisti bar complex. On the protected shoreward side the restricted marine Back-Bar facies was deposited and on the seaward side the open marine Fore-Bar facies accumulated. A basinward pulse of subsidence resulted in the burial of all these Gallup facies beneath the transgressive "Upper" Mancos Shale.

Table 3. Summary of Petrographic Characteristics, Bisti Area[1]

	Median Grain Size	Maximum Grain Size	Clay Matrix Content	Dolomite Grain Percent	Glauconite Content	Benthonic Forams	Planktonic Forams, Collophane, Inoceramus
Main Gallup Sandstone							
Beach sand	Medium to fine	Very coarse	Low	2 to 11	Trace to present	Trace	Absent
Offshore sand	Very fine	Medium to fine	Moderate	15 to 30	Absent to trace	Present	Trace
Low-SP facies	Fine to very fine	Very coarse to medium	Very high	5 to 20	Trace to present	Trace	Absent
Bar sands	Medium to fine	Very coarse to coarse	Low, but increases toward base	<5 restricted to basal part	Very abundant throughout	Trace	Absent, except on seaward flank
Backbar facies	Fine to very fine	Coarse to medium	High	5 to 15	Trace to present	Very abundant	Absent, except for displaced fragments
Forebar facies	Fine to very fine	Medium to fine	High	8 to 25	Trace to present	Common	Very abundant
"Upper" Mancos Shale	Very fine	Medium to fine	High	5 to 30	Absent to trace	Common	Very abundant

[1] After Sabins (1963).

Thus the Bisti stratigraphic trap was formed and preserved by marine depositional processes which may be deciphered through detailed study of the rocks.

MORROWAN SANDSTONES, ANADARKO BASIN

The reservoirs of the Morrowan Series of northwestern Oklahoma consist of a repetitious sequence of gas-bearing beach sandstones. All gas accumulations are in stratigraphic traps. The essentials of prospecting in this area were presented by Busch (1959, p. 2830–2832) in the early stages of drilling, but subsequent development drilling now affords an opportunity for a more detailed analysis. Figure 38 is a generalized south-north cross section (A-B) of the Morrowan (Lower Pennsylvanian) strata. The Morrowan strata form a genetic sequence of rocks lying unconformably on the Mississippian; this GSS is defined at the top by the base of the "Thirteen-Finger" limestone. The Morrowan represents a south-to-north transgressive unit with southward thickening that reflects the inclusion in that direction of progressively older beds at the base. Time lines are essentially parallel with the base of the "Thirteen-Finger" limestone and impinge against the truncated surface of the underlying Mississippian.

Three sandstones can be identified from the cross section in Figure 38. They bear an *en échelon* relation to each other, and each wedges out basinward to the south. The uppermost sandstone impinges against the old Mississippian land surface, whereas the lowest of the three sandstones wedges out before it reaches the unconformity. It cannot be determined from this profile whether the middle sandstone grades into shale before it reaches the unconformity. A more detailed

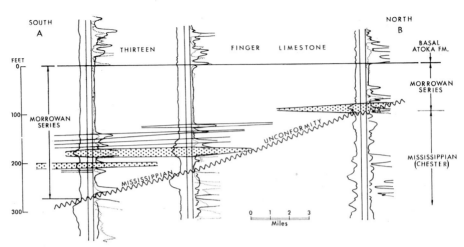

FIG. 38—Simplified stratigraphic profile *A-B* of Morrowan Series, northwestern Oklahoma, showing *en échelon* arrangement of three basal sandstone members. Location is shown on Figure 40. After Busch (1959).

cross section (A-B) is shown in Figure 39. This cross section was drawn at approximately the same position as that of Figure 38, but many more logs were used in its construction. Individual *en échelon* sandstone bodies are stippled. Most of the sandstones grade into either shale or siltstone in the direction of the unconformity. Basinward (south), several of the sandstones grade into siltstone. Each of these sandstone bodies was deposited during a stillstand of the shoreline under conditions of cyclic marine transgression of the Early Pennsylvanian sea. They consist of either an offshore bar or fringing beach sands, or both, and they trend parallel with the ancient shoreline positions. Each of the sandstones is a separate reservoir abundantly productive of gas.

An isopach map of the genetic sequence (Morrowan Series) containing the gas-producing sandstone members is shown in Figure 40. The Morrowan sequence represents more or less continuous sedimentation, although the shoreline was transgressing in a cyclic manner. In essence, this isopach map represents the simulated paleotopographic surface of the eroded Mississippian over which the Early Pennsylvanian sea transgressed. The known trends of individual sandstone members of the Morrowan are indicated by sinuous stippled

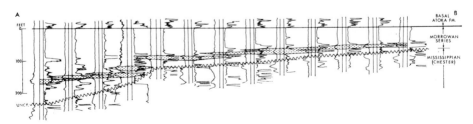

FIG. 39—Stratigraphic profile *A-B* of Morrowan Series, northwestern Oklahoma, showing *en échelon* onlap relation of reservoir sandstones. Location is shown on Figure 40. After Busch (1963).

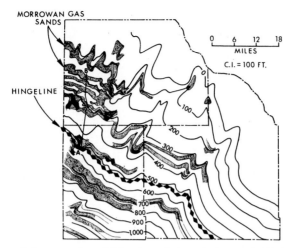

FIG. 40—Early isopach interpretation of Morrowan Series, northwestern Oklahoma, showing generalized trends of several gas-bearing sandstones (stippled). Note manner in which individual sandstones follow restricted thickness intervals of Morrowan. After Busch (1963).

bands. Each of these sandstones follows a different critical thickness interval of the genetic increment to which it is related. In all of this analysis the base of the "Thirteen-Finger" limestone is considered as an isochron essentially parallel with sea level. The basinward thickening of the Morrowan Series simulates the basinward slope of the unconformable Mississippian surface. Because this was an irregular surface, the cyclic shoreline trends were equally irregular, causing the sinuosity of the *en échelon*, "stairstep" sandstones.

Figure 41 (Khaiwka, 1968) was drawn approximately 5 years after Fig-

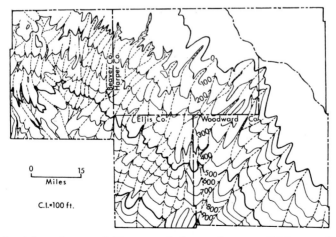

FIG. 41—Updated isopach map of Morrowan Series, northwestern Oklahoma, which simulates pre-Pennsylvanian paleotopographic surface; stream channels are indicated by dashed lines. After Khaiwka (1968).

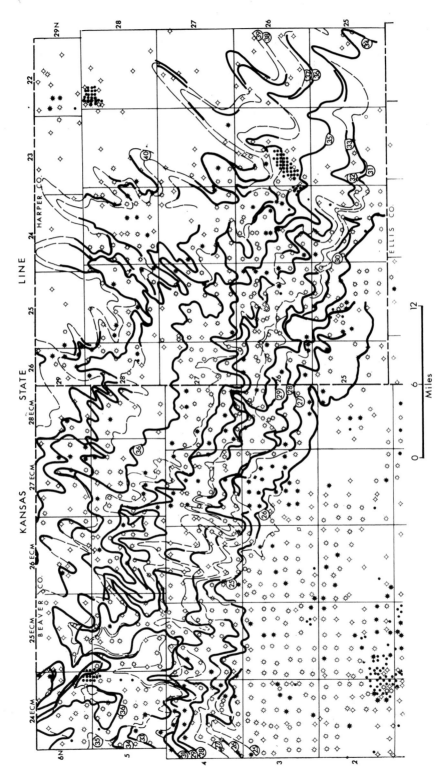

FIG. 42—Several successive stages of shoreline trends in Morrowan Series, northwestern Oklahoma. Heavy lines are shorelines with sand development; dashed lines are shorelines without sand development. After Khaiwka (1968).

ure 40, when more than twice as many log data were available. This isopach map (Fig. 41) of the Morrowan clearly shows the southwesterly-flowing pre-Pennsylvanian drainage courses which were eroded into the Mississippian surface. As an adjunct to this study, Khaiwka has identified every sandstone and siltstone unit within the Morrowan by number. The trends and positions of their respective northeastward wedge-outs are shown in Figure 42. In most of the area there is considerable overlap of several sandstones and siltstones; therefore, it is impossible to portray graphically the geographic extent of each sandstone. Most of the shoreline positions are represented by siltstone that terminates against the Mississippian unconformity surface. In several places, however, sandstone impinges against the unconformity. The shoreline trends of Figure 42 show striking parallelism with the simulated topographic configuration of the Mississippian (Fig. 41).

In Figure 43 the trends, thicknesses, and widths of three of the numbered Morrowan sandstone and siltstone members are shown. The landward (northern) margins of these sandstones parallel the shoreline. The irregularities of the seaward margins probably resulted from such variable factors as irregularities on the seafloor (caused partly by differential compaction), direction of wave motion, longshore currents, and delta positions. Sandstone 29 not only exhibits a very irregular, fringing beach sand, but also several subparallel offshore bars. This type of map can be constructed for each of the Morrowan sandstone members.

Figure 44 is a structure map of the Mississippian surface in northwestern Oklahoma. There is almost complete absence of structural closure. This surface has been tilted basinward (south) in post-Morrowan time, as indicated by steeper basinward dip than that of the paleotopographic surface shown in Figure 40. Also, the structural contour lines are less sinuous than the contours of the paleotopographic map.

In all the studies of the Morrowan sandstones, it has been possible to trace individual sandstone members systematically, as outlined above. These maps (Figs. 40–44), however, constitute only a geologic framework for systematic sampling, detailed thin-section studies, and other petrographic investigations. There should be diagnostic petrographic differences for the offshore-bar, fringing-beach, channel, and delta sandstones—all of which are present in the Morrowan Series. The maximum density of well control for these studies is one well per square mile. In the southeastern part of the study area, the density of well control is considerably less.

MESAVERDE SANDSTONES, SAN JUAN BASIN

Hollenshead and Pritchard (1961) published an analysis of the Mesaverde sandstones of the San Juan basin of New Mexico. Their most significant contribution is the step-by-step discussion of the methods employed in the subsurface stratigraphic analysis. Their paper, reviewed here, is a concrete application of fundamental principles of stratigraphy.

Large quantities of gas have been produced from sandstones at the bottom

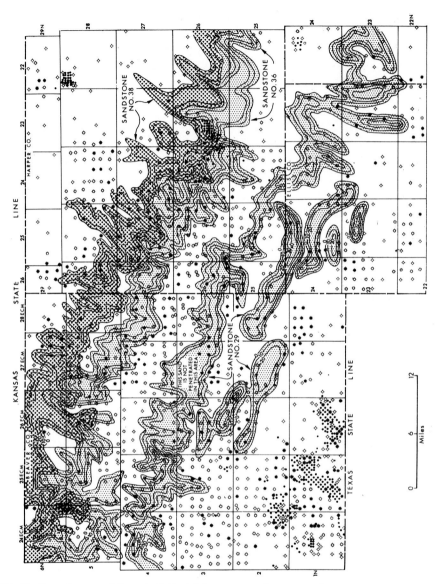

FIG. 43—Isopach map of three individual Morrowan sandstones, northwestern Oklahoma. After Khaiwka (1968).

and top of the Mesaverde Group. The accumulations are stratigraphic and bear no relation to structure.

The San Juan basin and the area of study of Hollenshead and Pritchard, relative to the Four Corners area, are shown in Figure 45. The gas-producing area is approximately 75 mi (120 km) long and 30 mi (48 km) wide and trends northwest-southeast. Approximately 1,900 electric and gamma ray–neutron logs, well cuttings, cores, and thin sections were used,

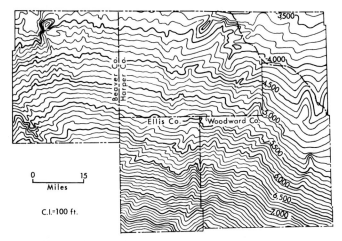

Fig. 44—Structure of top of Mississippian, northwestern Oklahoma. Note that axial trends of structural lows are similar to paleodrainage courses shown in Figure 41. After Khaiwka (1968).

The Mesaverde Group was deposited in middle Cretaceous time in a broad, shallow sea. The embayment extended for several thousand miles north-south and approximately 1,000 mi (1600 km) east-west. The western shoreline, in the Four Corners area, locally had a northwest-southeast trend. This shoreline fluctuated widely, first regressing and later transgressing. The San Juan basin is a closed structural basin which lies within a small part of the total area of middle Cretaceous strata. The configuration of this structural basin is reproduced from Hollenshead and Pritchard in Figure 51.

Figure 46 is a chart showing the named lithologic units deposited in Late Cretaceous time in the San Juan basin area. The lowest formation of the Mesaverde Group is the Point Lookout Sandstone. It consists of fine-grained to very fine-grained marine sandstone which contains considerable gas. The Menefee Formation is a northeastward-thinning wedge of continental strata consisting of nonmarine shale, sandstone, and coal; these beds are erratic and have no oil or gas. The Menefee Formation is overlain by the Cliff House Sandstone, which is fine- to very fine-grained sandstone and is gas bearing.

Fig. 45—Location of area studied by Hollenshead and Pritchard (1961) with respect to San Juan basin and Four Corners area.

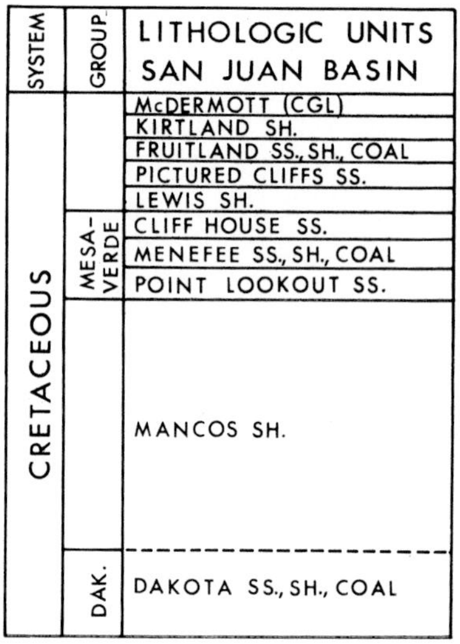

SYSTEM	GROUP	LITHOLOGIC UNITS SAN JUAN BASIN
CRETACEOUS	MESA-VERDE	McDERMOTT (CGL)
		KIRTLAND SH.
		FRUITLAND SS., SH., COAL
		PICTURED CLIFFS SS.
		LEWIS SH.
		CLIFF HOUSE SS.
		MENEFEE SS., SH., COAL
		POINT LOOKOUT SS.
		MANCOS SH.
	DAK.	DAKOTA SS., SH., COAL

FIG. 46—Named Upper Cretaceous lithologic units in San Juan basin area. Modified from Hollenshead and Pritchard (1961).

The stratigraphic and facies relations of these three formations are shown in the lower part of Figure 47. The Point Lookout Sandstone bears a regressive relation to time lines through approximately 350 ft (107 m) of section. The Cliff House Sandstone exhibits a transgressive relation through about 210 ft (64 m) of section (right to left, Fig. 47). Between the Point Lookout and Cliff House Sandstones, the Menefee thins from 860 ft (262 m) in the southwest to 160 ft (49 m) in the northeast. The marine Mancos Shale was deposited concurrently with the lower Menefee and the Point Lookout Sandstone, whereas the marine Lewis Shale was deposited during the transgressive phase of Cliff

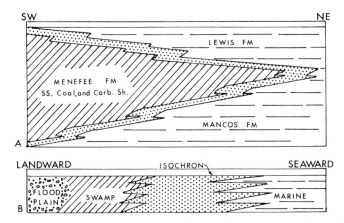

FIG. 47—**A.** Southwest-northeast cross section of Mesaverde in San Juan basin, showing time relation. **B.** Mesaverde depositional environments. After Hollenshead and Pritchard (1961).

House deposition. Thus, during the time of Mesaverde deposition, four depositional environments existed concurrently. They are illustrated diagrammatically in the lower part of Figure 47. They include a continental-floodplain environment which was separated from the shore- and nearshore-sand environment by a narrow, coal-forming swamp. Basinward from the marginal-marine environment, mud was being deposited. All four environments first regressed and then transgressed during the time of Mesaverde deposition. The different sediment types of each environment were deposited laterally in response to the shoreline movements. A thin coal bed directly overlies the Point Lookout Sandstone and another underlies the Cliff House Sandstone. Neither coal is a meaningful time reference datum. The landward margins of the two sandstones are abrupt where they are in contact with coal, whereas they grade laterally into the marine shale and siltstone on the seaward margin.

Three sets of conditions are illustrated in the upper part of Figure 47:

1. The rate of sedimentation exceeded the rate of subsidence, resulting in a regression of the shoreline.
2. The rate of subsidence predominated over the rate of sedimentation, resulting in a transgression of the shoreline.
3. The rates of sedimentation and subsidence were in equilibrium, resulting in a stillstand of the shoreline and a relatively thick, local accumulation of shoreline and nearshore sands.

Four stages of cyclic regression of the shoreline (Fig. 48) are recognized for the Point Lookout Sandstone by Hollenshead and Pritchard (1961). The Point Lookout is not a uniform blanket sandstone. It contains four local areas of thicker sandstone, each of which is the result of a stillstand of the overall regressive shoreline. These thicker areas consist of well-sorted sandstone, whereas the thinner, platformlike sandstone is poorly sorted. The latter was deposited in areas of comparatively rapid shoreline movement.

Figure 49 illustrates the three stages of cyclic subsidence that occurred during the time of deposition of the Cliff House Sandstone. Again, stillstands of the shoreline resulted in locally thicker accumulations of well-sorted sand, whereas comparatively rapid marine transgressions caused deposition of the poorly sorted, connecting sheet sandstones.

A lithologic marker bed in the lower part of the marine Lewis Shale was selected as a datum of reference. Lithologically, it consists of a bentonite zone which appears on the majority of the electric logs as a resistivity "low." Other usable markers are present in the few areas where this zone becomes obscure on the electric logs. The bentonite marker bed, referred to as the "green marker horizon," is parallel with the other resistivity "lows." In plotting cross sections, such as that shown in Figure 50, Hollenshead and Pritchard used the "green marker horizon" as the datum of reference; thereby, the upper and lower boundaries of the Menefee could be established readily. They reconstructed the depositional history of the Mesaverde in the restricted area of the San Juan structural basin. The Point Lookout and Cliff House sandstone benches are

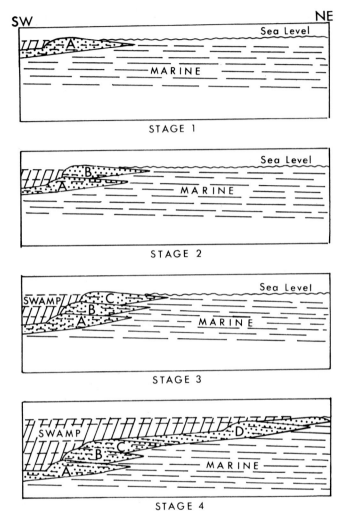

FIG. 48—Southwest-northeast cross sections, showing irregular regressive Point Lookout shoreline. After Hollenshead and Pritchard (1961).

directly related to steps in the strandline. The sandstone benches terminate abruptly in a landward (southwest) direction against the swamp deposits of the Menefee Formation. The seaward margins (northeast) of these benches are transitional and cannot be defined as easily as the landward margins.

Figure 51 is a structural map of the San Juan basin drawn on the "green marker horizon." A regional dip of approximately 1,500 ft (457 m) is mostly to the northeast. The overall picture is one of a very asymmetric syncline. Gas is trapped principally where sandstone grades into shale updip along the landward margins of the successive Point Lookout and Cliff House sandstone benches. Hollenshead and Pritchard constructed two isopach maps for the pur-

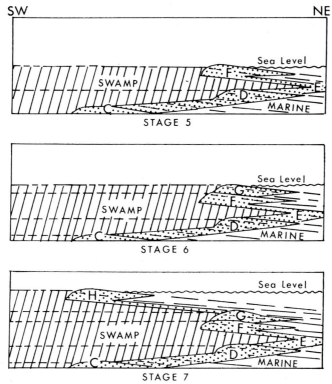

FIG. 49—Southwest-northeast cross sections, showing irregular transgressive Cliff House Sandstone. After Hollenshead and Pritchard (1961).

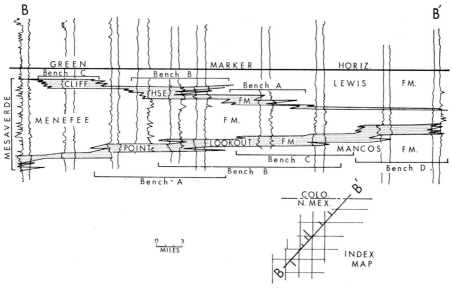

FIG. 50—Southwest-northeast cross section *B-B'*, showing stratigraphic relations of Mesaverde sandstones. After Hollenshead and Pritchard (1961).

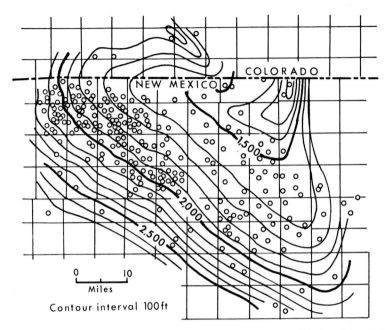

FIG. 51—Structure map, "green marker horizon," San Juan basin, New Mexico. After Hollenshead and Pritchard (1961).

pose of determining the depositional trends and widths of these benches. The first isopach map, shown in Figure 52, is of the stratigraphic interval from the "green marker horizon" down to the base of the Cliff House Sandstone. This is a genetic increment of strata similar to that illustrated diagrammatically in Figure 16C. More stable shoreline areas and trends are identified by closely spaced contour lines, whereas the areas of transgression are indicated by wide spacing of the thickness contours. Thus, the paleodepositional trends of the shoreline have been reconstructed by a technique which removes any effects of postdepositional tectonism. These shoreline trends are completely independent of the present-day structural configuration of the San Juan basin.

Figure 53 is an isopach map of a genetic sequence of strata with the "green marker horizon" at the top; the base of the Menefee was used as the bottom of the genetic sequence because of the sharp contact between a coal bed and the underlying Point Lookout Sandstone. Four distinct benches have been identified; they represent different stages of the regression that occurred during the time of Point Lookout deposition. The subsidence pulses were of a lesser order of magnitude than those which occurred during deposition of the Cliff House Sandstone. It is apparent that this technique of selective isopach mapping of genetic increments and genetic sequences of strata serves as a means of projecting shorelines into unexplored areas in which there is a minimum of subsurface well control. Lease plays, as well as the selection of specific drillsites, can be based on this type of subsurface stratigraphic analysis. In this instance, a knowl-

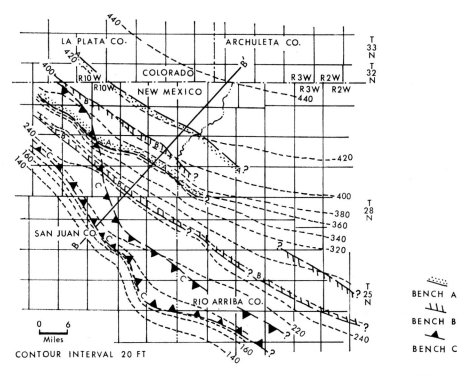

FIG. 52—Isopach map, "green marker horizon" to top of Menefee, showing principal Cliff House benches. After Hollenshead and Pritchard (1961).

edge of the structure of the area is of very little value from the standpoint of leasing and drilling.

Wanek (1954) mapped the trends of two benches (tongues) of Mesaverde sandstone in the outcrop area northwest of the San Juan basin. The trends and positions of these two benches are remarkably similar to those of the Cliff House benches B and C (Fig. 53). Similar benches, exposed at the surface, have been reported southeast of the San Juan basin. A surface stratigraphic study of the Mesaverde in the areas to the southeast and northwest of the San Juan basin, prior to the development of this extensive gas field, enabled one major company to project and correlate benches of sandstone across the area of the then-unknown subsurface equivalents. By "tying" together the outcrops and predicting the subsurface occurrence of these benches, this company was able to lease and drill considerably ahead of competition.

STRIKE-VALLEY SANDSTONES

The term "strike-valley sandstones" was proposed by Busch (1959, p. 2832) to designate those sandstones deposited in low areas between cuestas at the time the land surface is inundated by a transgressive sea. Such cuestas may be either erosional escarpments or fault scarps. Erosional escarpments are the result of

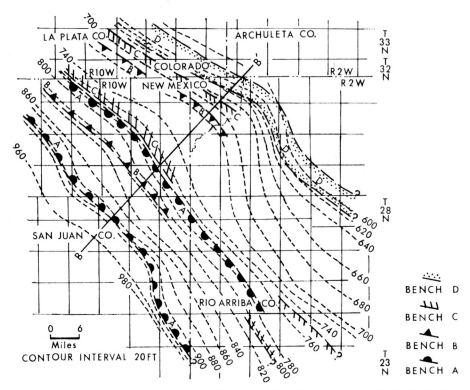

BENCH D

BENCH C

BENCH B

BENCH A

Fig. 53—Isopach map, "green marker horizon" to base of Menefee, showing principal Point Lookout benches. After Hollenshead and Pritchard (1961).

progressive truncation of a series of alternating resistant and nonresistant strata, all of which have been regionally tilted.

Strike-valley sandstones are unique in that they may be classified as either marginal-marine or channel sandstones. They were first defined and illustrated from an example in the Mid-Continent area. Since then, many examples have been identified by other geologists in other areas. Figure 54 shows the structural configuration of the Mississippian in a pool area where there is abundant sub-surface control. Well spacing is one well per 40 acres, and all of the control consists of electric-log data. The contour interval is 10 ft (3.0 m). A very narrow, apparently anticlinal ridge plunges westward along the southern border of the mapped area. There is a conspicuous, narrow, westward-plunging asymmetric trough adjacent on the north. This is not a true structure map; rather, it represents a combination of post-Mississippian topography and structure, the latter imposed by post-Pennsylvanian tilting. There is a direct relation of this surface to the distribution of a lenticular sandstone which overlies it. The maximum thickness of this sandstone is 50–55 ft (15.2–16.8 m).

Figure 55 is two north-south cross sections of the same body of sandstone that produces from the pool shown in Figure 54. The cross section in the upper half of the figure is drawn with a limestone datum of reference; the limestone

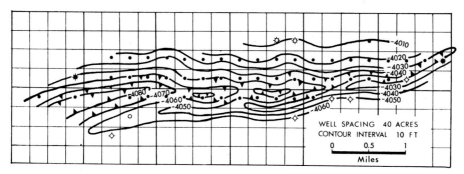

FIG. 54—Structural configuration of Mississippian, showing synclinal position of an overlying strike-valley sandstone. After Busch (1959).

is a time marker that is persistent and easily recognized. The Mississippian unconformity is indicated by a wavy line not parallel with the limestone datum. This unconformity shows progressive truncation northward, but a thin, resistant limestone escarpment is present just basinward from the southernmost producing well in the pool. The sandstone body, shaded black, is very asymmetric in cross section, having a teardrop profile. The relation of a strike-valley sandstone body to this combination of topographic and structural surface is more than a coincidence. The lower half of Figure 55 illustrates the same condition as that shown in the upper half, except that it has been drawn with sea level as datum. The lenticular sandstone slopes at an angle similar to the slope of the Mississippian surface, but it wedges out abruptly near the escarpment.

Figure 56 is a block diagram illustrating the deposition of the strike-valley sandstone. During sea-level position 1, the shoreline was in the middle of the block diagram and the lower body of sandstone (shaded black) was accumulating on the escarpment side of the more seaward ridge. As the surface of deposition was transgressed, the shoreline shifted from right to left (south to north) and a second body of sandstone was deposited behind the next higher topographic escarpment. From a diagram of this type it is apparent that the top of the Mississippian is not a true structural surface, but is a combination of structure

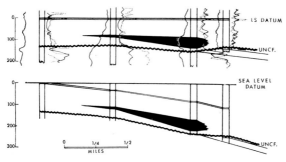

FIG. 55—North-south profiles, showing relation of a strike-valley sandstone to underlying pre-Pennsylvanian erosion surface After Busch (1959).

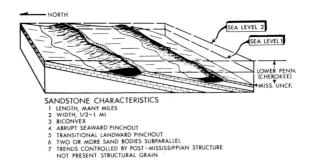

SANDSTONE CHARACTERISTICS
1 LENGTH, MANY MILES
2 WIDTH, 1/2–1 MI
3 BICONVEX
4 ABRUPT SEAWARD PINCHOUT
5 TRANSITIONAL LANDWARD PINCHOUT
6 TWO OR MORE SAND BODIES SUBPARALLEL
7 TRENDS CONTROLLED BY POST–MISSISSIPPIAN STRUCTURE
  NOT PRESENT STRUCTURAL GRAIN

FIG. 56—Block diagram, illustrating relation of strike-valley sandstones to erosional escarpments developed on tilted and truncated Mississippian surface. After Busch (1959).

and paleotopography. This type of surface, when inundated, controls the sites, trends, and linearity of the sands deposited.

The geometry of a sandstone of this type may be summarized as follows:

1. The lengths of the individual bodies of sandstone may be many miles.

2. The widths may vary from ½ to 1 mi (0.8–1.6 km) or more, depending on the angularity of the depositional slope.

3. The cross section is asymmetrically biconvex with an abrupt seaward transition into shale and a gradual landward pinchout.

4. Two or more such sand bodies are generally subparallel. Their trends are controlled by the original predepositional topography and not by the present structural grain of the strata beneath the unconformity.

Inasmuch as a strike-valley sand is deposited in the drainage course of a subsequent stream valley, the sand body will have an initial slope in the direction of stream flow. The direction of flow and the paleogradient of a strike valley can be determined by constructing an isopach map of the genetic increment of strata between a lithologic time marker above the sandstone and the unconformity below the sandstone. Such a GIS will thicken systematically in a downstream direction, and the rate of thickening (in feet per mile) will approximate the paleogradient.

The first stream to develop on a newly uplifted coastal plain flows in a direction essentially perpendicular to the shoreline of the bordering embayment. Such a stream is a consequent stream. It will lengthen as a result of headwater erosion and, thereby, will cut a valley through both hard and soft rock. The first tributaries to develop will erode in the softer rock and flow into the master (consequent) stream essentially at right angles. These tributaries are subsequent streams which erode strike valleys. Thus, two subsequent streams may occupy the same strike valley, behind an escarpment, and flow in opposite directions toward each other. Both of them will join the consequent stream at approximately the same point. When such a strike valley later becomes clogged with sand as a result of a marine transgression, the resulting strike-valley sandstone may be within a genetic increment which exhibits thickening in two opposite directions. At the point of maximum thickness of such a genetic increment, it may be anticipated that a cross-trending channel sandstone will be present. This channel sandstone represents a clogging of the consequent stream channel. Such clogging may be brought about by an upstream shift in the base level of deposition of the consequent stream as it gradually is inundated by the marine transgression. The origin of a sand-filled strike valley, however, is not explained as readily. Such a valley also may be filled as the base level shifts upstream during marine transgression. However, a more likely explanation for the origin of a strike-valley sand is transportation of marginal-marine sands by longshore currents after the bordering landmass is inundated.

The practical applications of reconstructing paleogeomorphology are discussed in detail in a scholarly paper by Martin (1966).

6

channel sandstones

Numerous types of sandstone bodies encountered in the subsurface have two characteristics in common—they are elongate and lenticular in cross section. These characteristics apply to sandstones resulting from fringing-beach, offshore-bar, chenier, strike-valley, sand-wave, tidal-current, and channel deposition, as well as to some turbidites and some component parts of deltas. Of all these types of sandstone, the channel type is very unusual in that it commonly is deposited subaerially and thus can be observed and studied more readily on the surface. In recent years, many pertinent papers dealing with outcropping ancient channel sandstones have been published. The reader is referred particularly to the following authors for basic information: Fisk (1944), Wilson (1948), Lins (1950), Siever (1951), Pepper *et al.* (1954), Hopkins (1958), Friedman (1960), Schlee and Moench (1961), Andresen (1961, 1962), Potter (1962a), Potter and Pettijohn (1963), and Bernard and Major (1963).

DRAINAGE SYSTEMS

The petroleum exploration geologist working with subsurface channel sandstones must have a background knowledge of geomorphology and subsurface techniques. An individual channel is almost invariably a component part of a drainage system. A detailed analysis of an individual subsurface channel sandstone generally will lead to other reservoirs which are genetically related.

Drainage systems are of various types. Perhaps the most common type is the *dendritic* pattern of drainage, in which the tributaries bifurcate at acute angles, forming treelike branches. Such a drainage system generally is developed in homogeneous, layered rock that is rather uniformly resistant to weathering and erosion. The bedrock is essentially horizontal and of a single lithology. In a *trellis* drainage pattern, subparallel streams follow the strike of the strata, which have been tilted or folded. Alternating hard and soft strata are exposed sub-aerially as a result of the tilting, and the subparallel drainage courses are eroded into the softer strata. A *rectangular* drainage pattern resembles a trellis pattern except that tributaries join the main stream essentially at right angles. In this case, a main stream has cut its channel across both the hard and soft rock, which previously had been tilted. Other names that apply to individual streams making up component parts of a rectangular drainage system are *consequent, subsequent, resequent,* and *obsequent.* The subsurface significance and identification of these stream types were described and illustrated by Martin (1966). A *barbed* pattern is one in which tributaries join the main stream at an angle greater than 90 degrees. This situation is not common. In an area of "dump" topography, such as a ground, recessional, or terminal moraine, the drainage may be *deranged,* having no apparent systematic control other than the initial depressions on the original surface. This type of drainage has no significance in subsurface studies of channels. Other drainage patterns which are uncommon in the subsurface are *centripetal, radial,* and *annular.* The most common drainage patterns in the subsurface are the dendritic, trellis, and rectangular.

Individual channels may be straight, crooked, contorted, meandering, anastomosing, or braided, or may consist of a deltaic system of distributaries. The latter is of such importance as to merit separate treatment. It generally is possible to determine from subsurface data not only the type of drainage pattern, but also related information such as paleogradient and direction of stream flow. The practical significance of this type of information is discussed later in this treatment of channel sandstones.

Cross Sections of Ancient Channel Sandstones

To recognize and trace ancient channel sandstones in the subsurface, the exploration geologist must acquire a background knowledge of all the known cross-sectional shapes and the methods of delineating and projecting them. Figure 57 diagrammatically illustrates six channel-fill situations and their normal appearance on the electric log. The caption for each is meant to be as descriptive as possible.

Postcompaction Cut and Fill

Figure 57A illustrates the type of channel-fill profile that is formed where the substrata have been compacted thoroughly (by weight of overburden) prior to uplift and erosion. The channel is filled with noncompactible sand, or with sand and gravel. Where the subjacent and lateral strata (usually shale) previously have been compacted, the fill exhibits a planoconvex profile, even after considerable overburden is deposited. The electric log commonly will have a bell-shaped profile, indicating a sharp basal contact of the coarser detritus with the underlying rocks. There is a general decrease in grain size upward. The upper part of the fill may be a silty zone transitional with the overlying shale, or it may be interbedded fine-grained sandstone and shale. In either case, the upper boundary of the fill commonly is difficult to identify from the electric log. The

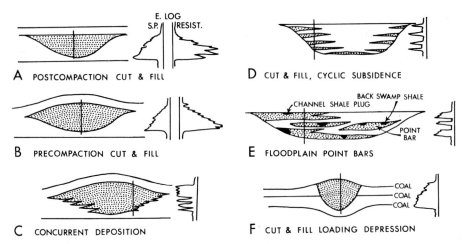

Fɪɢ. 57—Schematic diagrams of six types of channel-fill situations encountered in subsurface.

electric log should be used as a supplemental tool, and never as the sole criterion for identifying a channel sandstone in the subsurface.

The channel fill may consist of both horizontal and crossbedded sandstone. The texture may range from a pebbly conglomerate at the base to a very fine-grained sandstone elsewhere in the channel. Coarser textured sandstone and pebbly conglomerate also may be present at various positions within the main body of the fill. Sorting generally is poor to fair. In many places the fill consists of discrete zones of well-sorted to poorly sorted sandstone interbedded and interlaminated with siltstone. Distinct shale "breaks" and pockets also may make up a part of the channel fill. It even is possible for all of the fill to consist of shale and silty shale. In this case, the electric log is of very limited value in subsurface identification and the bell-shaped profile does not apply. A shale fill of a channel can be identified from the electric log, however, if the channel is in bedrock consisting principally of either sandstone or limestone.

Precompaction Cut and Fill

Figure 57B is the type of channel-fill profile that is created if the channel is eroded prior to or during compaction. The internal characteristics of the fill material generally are the same as those indicated for postcompaction fill (Fig. 57A). The electric log, likewise, is similar to that of Figure 57A, provided the fill material is principally sandstone. The phenomenon of differential compaction is a complicating factor when analyzing this type of sandstone in the subsurface. Sand undergoes very little, if any, compaction due to the weight of the over-burden, whereas the laterally adjacent shales ultimately can compact to 45–55 percent of their original depositional thickness.

Figure 58 is a schematic illustration of the stages leading to this type of channel-fill profile. Stage A shows a channel eroded into partially compacted clay and shale. In Stage B the channel is filled with sand to height "H" and the

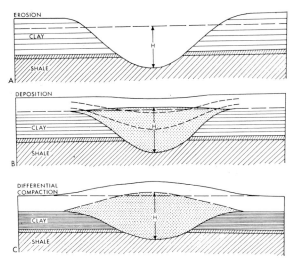

FIG. 58—Schematic stages of erosion, deposition, and differential compaction of sediments related to a channel sandstone.

entire area is blanketed with a thin layer of overburden. The downwarped dashed lines are isochrons indicating that the upper part of the overburden may be deposited concurrently with the channel-fill sand. In Stage C the channel is completely filled with sand and the laterally adjacent clay and shale are compacted to approximately two thirds of their original thickness. The fact that differential compaction is concurrent with deposition of the channel fill and the overburden is indicated by the slight thinning of the overburden in the area directly above the position of maximum sand thickness. The most significant feature of this illustration is the thickening of the sand primarily at the expense of the underlying clay and shale and not at the expense of the overlying beds. This is a diagnostic criterion for identification of a channel sandstone in the subsurface. This criterion alone usually will serve to distinguish a channel-fill sandstone from an offshore bar in the subsurface. The latter type of sandstone body usually thickens primarily at the expense of the overburden. In making such a determination it is best to select several closely spaced electric logs which exhibit sharply contrasting thicknesses of sandstone. If a lithologic marker bed below the fill is selected as the datum of reference in constructing a stratigraphic profile, then any similar marker bed a short distance above the channel fill will be bowed upward (owing to differential compaction) if the fill consists principally of sandstone. However, the interval of shale which separates the top of the sandstone from the upper marker bed will remain fairly persistent in thickness except for a slight local thinning directly above the thickest portion of the lenticular sandstone.

It generally is more meaningful to restore the lense of sandstone to its original cross-sectional shape, and this is accomplished by selecting a lithologic reference datum above the sandstone. By this means, the reference datum is restored to its original depositional attitude and the top of the channel sandstone, likewise, is flattened. Such a restoration of the original sandstone profile, however, will cause any lithologic marker beds a short distance below the sandstone to be distorted out of their depositional attitude and to be bowed downward. Regardless of whether a reference datum is selected above the lense of channel sandstone or below it, the thickening of the sandstone is accomplished primarily at the expense of the subjacent strata.

Concurrent Deposition

Figure 57C is an example of concurrent deposition in which the channel fills with sand at the same time that the laterally adjacent areas are receiving mud and silt. The diagnostic criteria for this type of channel fill are the same as those for precompaction cut and fill (Fig. 57B) plus the interbedding of silty sandstone with the laterally adjacent shale. The electric log exhibits interbedded sandstone and shale in the basal part of the fill and shows mostly sandstone in the upper part. It will exhibit only sandstone, however, if the well happens to be situated in the center of the channel.

Two environmental situations are conducive to the development of this type of channel fill. One is the topset environment of a delta where distributary channels characteristically are present. As the channels periodically overflow their banks, a thin veneer of silts and clays is deposited in the back-swamp interdistributary areas. Thus, the deltaic plain is built up concurrently with a sand fill in the distributary channels. Such channel sands are not to be confused with the bar-finger sands described and illustrated by Fisk (1955, p. 8, 9) for the bird-foot delta of the Mississippi River.

Another environment in which this type of concurrent deposition occurs is where terrestrial sediments are discharged into shallow-marine waters and deposited on an irregular submarine surface. As an example, growth structures on the shallow seafloor are known to have existed in abundance along the Gulf Coast area in Tertiary and Quaternary time. These structures produced submarine topographic irregularities which, in turn, caused a localization of discharge water between and around submarine "highs." Sediment transported through the submarine "lows" was sand, silt, and clay. Sand-size material was deposited in the lows, and it interfingered with clay- and silt-size materials which were deposited concurrently in the quieter water along the margins of the lows and over the mounds separating the lows. Variations in the volumetric discharge of the sediments resulted in lateral interbedding of channel sandstone with clay and silt. The distributary pattern is not that of a true delta, but is somewhat haphazard owing to the irregular distribution of the submarine topographic highs.

An excellent example of the influence of growth structures in the development of the concurrent type of channel fill is illustrated in Figure 59. The concurrent submarine channel fill occurs just below a *Bolivina perca* faunal zone which was used as the reference datum for this illustration. This datum coincides perfectly with the base of a shale marker bed. Interval thicknesses above the sandstone

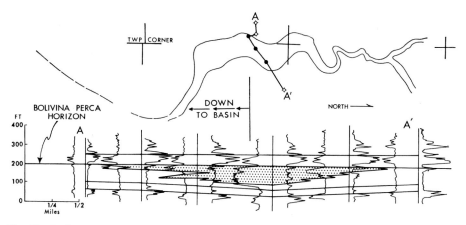

FIG. 59—Profile of an Anahuac (Oligocene-Miocene) channel sandstone, Acadia Parish, Louisiana, drawn to a *Bolivina perca* reference datum. Furnished by R. E. Slingerland (personal commun., 1967).

are remarkably uniform. The basal part of the sandstone interfingers with laterally adjacent shale, and the Anahuac reservoir sandstone increases in thickness at the expense of the subjacent shale. Because the *Bolivina perca* reference datum is restored arbitrarily to its original flattened condition, the two marker beds below the lenticular sandstone are bowed downward. The lack of parallelism of the two marker beds below the sandstone with the *Bolivina perca* reference datum is clear-cut proof of the differential compaction of the shales laterally adjacent to the channel sandstone. A plan view of the oil pool that produces from the Anahuac is shown in the upper part of Figure 59. It has the configuration of a channel, and the basinward direction is south. This channel can be traced for a considerable distance farther south. An isopach map of a genetic increment in this area might be constructed using the *Bolivina perca* datum as the upper marker bed and either of the correlated marker beds below the sandstone as the lower limit of the increment. On such a map, areas of maximum thickness will be coincident with maximum Anahuac sandstone development. The entire genetic increment consists of shale on both sides of the sandstone. This shale interval will have a minimum thickness above the growth structures that existed on the seafloor during Anahuac deposition. Mapping of the variations in thickness of this genetic increment makes it possible to reconstruct the submarine topography that existed during the time of Anahuac deposition.

The sandstone development can be inferred reasonably in the areas of the lows (thickest genetic increment). It is not to be expected that oil or gas will be present everywhere the sandstone in the Anahuac is developed. Rather, it will be located in restricted updip parts of the sandstone that result from domal uplift and growth faulting. Thus, a structure map of this *Bolivina perca* datum should be constructed and superimposed on the map of predicted Anahuac sandstone distribution as a basis for defining updip stratigraphic traps in this formation.

Cut and Fill Plus Cyclic Subsidence

A most unusual condition of channel fill is shown in Figure 57D. The channel is saucer shaped, indicating a mature stage of development. The dominant lithology of the channel fill is shale and silty shale, and this is interrupted on the flanks of the channel by several pairs of sandstone bodies which wedge out toward the center of the channel. A lense of sandstone also may be seen at the base of the channel. The wedges of sandstone on either side of the channel bear an *en échelon* relation to each other and are separated by distinct shale "breaks." Stratigraphically higher wedges appear in an upstream direction in profiles of a channel; conversely, the stratigraphically lower units disappear progressively upstream. The electric log of a well drilled on the edge of such a channel fill will record several thin sandstones separated by shale "breaks." The electric log of a well drilled in the central part of such a channel usually shows a single sandstone which occurs at the base of the fill and lies on the unconformity.

The distribution of sandstones along the flanks of the valley is interpreted as the result of a special combination of environmental circumstances. Immediately after the development of a broad floodplain eroded in soft shales, cyclic marine transgression occurred over the entire area. The stream that produced this broad valley was transporting vastly greater quantities of silt and mud than sand. At each stillstand of the shoreline, a fringing beach sand was deposited on both sides of the drowned valley. Such beach sands probably are the result of the winnowing action of waves acting on sediments furnished to the floodplain principally by bordering sheetwash. Only very restricted portions of such lenticular sandstones can be expected to contain hydrocarbons. The methods of mapping the trends and distribution of such sandstones, and of defining drillable prospects in such a situation, are described and illustrated in the discussion of the Muddy sandstones of the Powder River basin of northeastern Wyoming (under "Ancient Examples of Channel Fill").

Floodplain Point Bar

In any stream which has reached grade, where deposition and erosion are occurring simultaneously, point bars will be formed. Point bars are deposited by aggrading and meandering streams. Such features are deposited on the slip-off slope of a meandering stream, where the velocity is minimal. The cross section of deposits resulting from such a situation is illustrated in Figure 57E. Given sufficient time, the radii of curvature of individual meanders decrease as the stream erodes laterally (on the outside of the curve). Concurrently, but at a lesser rate, the individual meanders migrate in the direction of the slope of the floodplain which they produce. Many looping meanders are cut off, or abandoned, during high-water stages, and thus become separated from the main drainage course. Such abandoned meanders become oxbow lakes, which later are sites for accumulation of silt, mud, and vegetal material. In the earlier stages of meander development the point bars will have crescent shapes and will be located at staggered positions on either side of the stream. As the individual

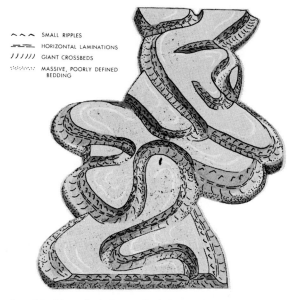

⌃ ⌃ ⌃   SMALL RIPPLES

⎯ ⎯ ⎯   HORIZONTAL LAMINATIONS

⫽⫽⫽⫽⫽   GIANT CROSSBEDS

⌁⌁⌁⌁⌁   MASSIVE, POORLY DEFINED
         BEDDING

FIG. 60—Drawing of model of hypothetical meander belt, showing how a complex point-bar reservoir sandstone would appear with clay plugs and surrounding material stripped away. Distribution of bedding structures is generalized. Zonation tends to follow this arrangement for a complete sequence. One or more of upper zones can be eroded away during later stages of meander development and a new sequence (or sequences) deposited on top. Plaster model prepared by John R. Warne (personal commun., 1967).

meanders become open loops, the point bars lose their crescent shapes and assume very irregular shapes, as illustrated in Figure 60. This illustration is a drawing of the actual model. The model illustrates the extremely irregular outline of a composite point-bar system such as might be anticipated in the subsurface. The width of the meander belt is much greater than the looping of any of the meanders of the stream. The complexities in exploring for oil and gas in this type of reservoir can best be appreciated by tilting the model so that the oil and gas migrate updip and are trapped in the structurally highest parts of each of the numerous point bars. The base of the model consists of a continuous stratum of poorly bedded coarse sandstone or conglomerate; thus, there would be a single reservoir-fluid system. The outlines of no two pools would be alike, and the updip margins in each case would be defined by the sinuosity of an impermeable mud-filled channel.

In spite of the irregularities of the plan view of the point-bar type of sandstone reservoir, the vertical profile is such that most point bars can be identified readily from single unoriented cores, regardless of the geologic age. The vertical profile of a point bar characteristically consists of four zones, which are diagrammatically illustrated in Figure 61. These zones, from the base upward, consist of (1) poorly bedded sand or gravel, (2) giant-ripple cross-stratification, (3) horizontally laminated beds, and (4) small ripples.

The basal zone of poorly bedded sand and gravel contains the largest grain

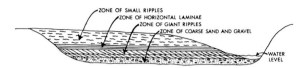

Fig. 61—Idealized cross section of a point bar, showing four fairly distinct zones commonly present as a result of different energy levels of stream. In general, grain size decreases progressively upward. Repetitions of graded series commonly occur; pebble bands are present at "perched" position within a composite section.

sizes of any of the four zones of a point bar. The size range varies greatly, depending on the size of detrital material available within a given drainage system. Other variables, such as stream gradient, composition of detrital material, volume of stream flow, *etc.,* play a part in determining the range of particle sizes present in this zone. With such variables, particle size can range from silt to boulder; the most common size range is medium to coarse sand and pebbles.

The zone of giant-ripple cross-stratification is directly above the normal low-water level of the stream and is deposited on the slip-off slope of the meanders during high-water stages of the stream. The individual cross-stratified layers range from a few inches to several feet in thickness. Clay inclusions and carbonized plant fragments commonly are present in cores of this zone. The uppermost boundary of this zone commonly is truncated and is overlain directly by the zone of horizontally laminated beds.

This latter zone is deposited during the periodic higher water stages of the stream as it expands beyond the confines of its usual channel course. It generally consists of fairly well-sorted, fine-grained sand which is interlaminated and interstratified with either very fine-grained sand or silt. Irregular clay nodules and carbonized plant stems and leaves also have been observed in cores of this zone. This zone is likely to have better horizontal than vertical permeability under subsurface reservoir conditions, owing to its laminated character.

The zone of small ripples is deposited only during flood stages of a stream and generally is the thickest of the four zones of a point bar. Also, it generally is the best sorted and finest textured zonal component of a point bar. The texture commonly is in the fine- to very fine-sand range. Few of the profuse small ripples exceed ⅛–¼ in. (0.32–0.64 cm) in amplitude. Irregular clay nodules and carbonized plant stems and leaves have been observed in cores of this zone. Horizontal and vertical permeabilities generally are similar.

In a few places, the normal sequence of zones in a point bar is interrupted by the presence of the basal, poorly bedded sand and gravel zone lying unconformably on either the zone of horizontally laminated beds or the uppermost zone of small ripples. This interrupted sequence is interpreted as the result of partial erosion of a normal point-bar sequence during a later stage of lateral erosion and deposition by the meandering stream. In other places, the complete sequence of zones may be developed several times within a single core. Such cores have been recovered and studied from channel fills in the Maracaibo basin of Venezuela.

The SP (spontaneous potential) curve of the electric log run through a single point bar generally exhibits a bell-shaped profile. This profile is due to a general decrease in grain size upward through a point bar, and is accompanied by a general increase in the percentage of clay from the base up. These characteristics are consistent with the fact that the energy of the environment decreases progressively upward through the four lithologic zones discussed.

Inasmuch as point bars make up only a part of the total sedimentary fill of a floodplain deposit, they are difficult to interpret in the subsurface. Although there is still much to be learned about methods of prospecting for such reservoirs, several steps will assist in identifying them in the subsurface. It was pointed out that a point bar can be identified from a single unoriented core by its four-part zonation. An isopach map of such a body of sand will exhibit a very abrupt decrease in thickness at the edge where it is in contact with a clay-filled channel. The outline of a point bar will have one or more smooth-curving margins defined by dry holes directly offsetting good production. An isopach map of the shale interval between the top of the sandstone and a lithologic reference datum above the sandstone will reveal abrupt changes in thickness caused by differential compaction of the silt and clay in the meandering channels. A structure map of this reference datum will show a draping effect around the margins of the sandstone body. Other techniques currently are under study, but they require more application and testing before appearing in print.

The Little Creek field of Lincoln and Pike Counties, Mississippi, shows enough of the gross geometric features of a point bar to leave little doubt regarding the origin of the reservoir sandstone. This field, which produces from the lower part of the Tuscaloosa sandstone (Upper Cretaceous), is estimated to have an ultimate yield of 25,000,000 bbl of oil (Eisenstatt, 1960). Figure 62 is an isopach map of the producing sandstone of this pool (Eisenstatt, 1960, p. 210); it illustrates the extremely irregular shape and thickness of the sandstone. The positions of dry holes which closely border the pool are especially significant. Sandstone 20–45 ft (6.1–13.7 m) thick grades completely into shale between wells drilled on 10-acre spacing. Eisenstatt (1960, p. 211) stated, "The sand can be fairly thick in one test and absent in another only a few feet away. This phenomenon is important since it is affecting the development of the Field to the extent that many of the holes were drilled as exceptions to field rules in order to find the edge of the sand body on a 40-acre unit." Logs of two wells spaced less than 660 ft (201 m) apart are shown in Figure 63. The "Denkman" sandstone* (the producing zone of the Tuscaloosa) of the Jones No. 2 well is totally absent in the Jones No. 1 well. These two wells are labeled on Figure 62. The position and trend of a postulated clay-filled channel have been superimposed by the writer on Figure 62. Figure 64 is a structure map prepared by Eisenstatt (1960) depicting his interpretation of the configuration of the "Lower Tuscaloosa" sandstone. He stated that, "The data shows [sic] a gentle south plunging nose. Only about 30 feet

---

* This sandstone should not be confused with the Jurassic Denkman Sandstone Member of the Norphlet Formation, which also is an important reservoir in this general area.

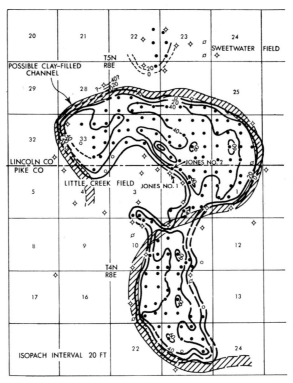

Fig. 62—Isopach map of "Denkman" sandstone of Little Creek field, Lincoln and Pike Counties, Mississippi, showing position and trend of a postulated clay-filled channel. Modified after Eisenstatt (1960).

of counter-regional north dip is present from the highest well to the lowest north flank producer. However, an oil column of about 110 feet is known to be present. From this it is concluded that this is a combination structural-stratigraphic trap."

Cut and Fill Plus Loading Depression

A last type of channel situation is that of cut and fill together with loading depression; it is illustrated in Figure 57F. This example and ideas pertaining to it are borrowed largely from Burnham's (1956) unpublished paper. The "I4 to K" stratigraphic interval represents a portion of the Oficina sandstones which were deposited on the shelf of the southern flank of the western Venezuela structural basin. The depositional environment during Oficina deposition was a combination of paludal, lagoonal, and brackish-marine conditions favorable for the development of extensive coal-forming swamps. It is an area in which there were numerous cyclic changes in either sea level or land level, resulting in a very thick alternating series of shales and complex intervals of coarser clastic beds. This was the site of a large distributary-delta system which deposited its sediments partly in a coastal subaerial environment and partly in a very shallow subaqueous environment. Innumerable distributary channels were eroded into semiconsolidated muds. Burnham stated:

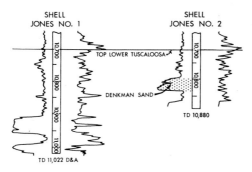

FIG. 63—Stratigraphic profile of part of lower Tuscaloosa sandstone, showing abrupt pinchout of "Denkman" sandstone in two wells approximately 250 ft apart; Little Creek field, Pike County, Mississippi. After Eisenstatt (1960).

With a slight rise in relative water level, the current velocity in the scour channels would be reduced and the channels would start back-filling with sand from behind sand bars at the mouths. This would result in "plugging with well-sorted sand channel fillings which make up narrow thick sand bodies characteristic of the shoal-water delta" (Fisk). The end result would be a channel almost choked with clean, well-sorted sand with a sluggish current depositing silts and silty shales in the upper part.

Burnham pointed out that these channel sands, ". . . are younger than the missing correlation markers that they have cut out and replaced." He stressed the fact that key marker beds, such as lignites, are structurally depressed (*i.e.,* they sag) beneath all trends of thick channel-sand development. This sag of the subjacent beds is accomplished without much thinning except where they have been eroded. In Figure 57F, only the middle one of the three lignite beds is not deformed.

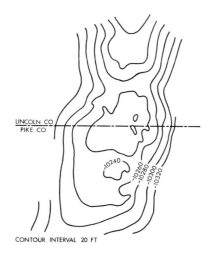

FIG. 64—Structure map, top of lower Tuscaloosa sandstone, Little Creek field, Lincoln and Pike Counties, Mississippi. After Eisenstatt (1960).

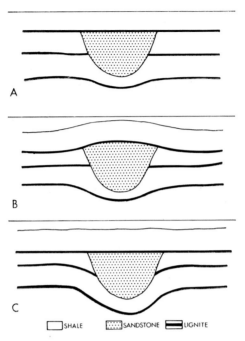

SHALE   SANDSTONE   LIGNITE

FIG. 65—Stages in development of cut-and-fill loading compaction associated with channels. After
Burnham (1956).

The upper lignite bed is convex upward owing to differential compaction of the
clays laterally adjacent to the sand-filled channel, whereas the lower lignite bed
is depressed owing to the concentrated load of sand directly above. The stages
in the development of this type of loading depression are illustrated in Figure 65.
Burnham (1956) postulated, ". . . that the underlying sediments were semi-
consolidated when these were formed, and not underlying soft clays as described
by Fisk. Semi-consolidated underlying sediments would spread the strain vertically
and horizontally, giving sag rather than squeezing or flowage."

A 175-ft (53 m) stratigraphic profile involving six wells is illustrated in
Figure 66. The reference datum is the I6 lignite zone at the top of the profile.
The J3a siltstone and the top of the J3b zone are sharply depressed by loading
compaction in areas directly beneath the two deep, sand-filled channels. It is the
writer's opinion that this type of cut-and-fill loading depression of subjacent
marker beds is much more likely to occur in a deltaic environment, where prodelta
muds are deposited in abundance, than in a strictly subaerial depositional environment.

INTERNAL STRUCTURE

It has been pointed out that there is considerable variability in the types of
sediment that might be deposited within a channel. In fact, practically every
type of sedimentary rock, except evaporites, may make up the lithology of a
channel fill. Grain size, degree of sorting, and cross-stratification are almost

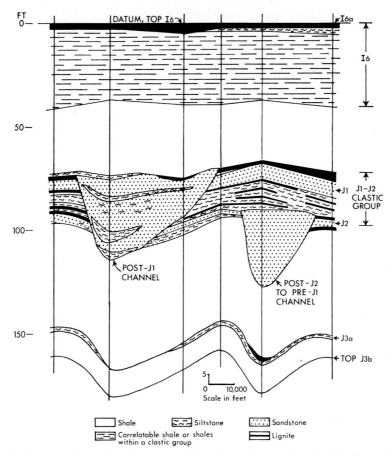

FIG. 66—Stratigraphic profile of part of Oficina Formation at East Mapiri, Maracaibo basin, Venezuela, showing cut-and-fill loading depressions of J3a and top of J3b zones below positions of maximum channel fill. After Burnham (1956).

as variable as the lithology. In some flume experiments performed by McKee (1957), some information has been gained on the factors influencing stratification. His experiments involved the deposition of fill in channels cut by (1) streams and (2) submarine (submerged) currents. It was noted that ". . . channels cut by streams tend to be flat bottomed, steep sided to straight walled, and shallow." Those cut by submarine currents ". . . are semi-circular in cross section as a result of constant slumping of the walls under water."

On the basis of these experiments, considerable significance can be attached to the position of water level as a determinative factor in the development of cross-stratification in a channel fill. McKee (1957, p. 133) showed that, ". . . where a stream deposits sediment in a channel bottom, as a result either of increase in stream load or decrease in stream velocity, the layering tends to be essentially horizontal so that it conforms to the flat-bottomed profile of scour in a stream-cut channel." This situation is shown in Figure 67A, which is the tracing of a photograph included in McKee's paper. In a completely water-filled channel, the layering of channel deposits may be concave upward. McKee stated that ". . . varying degrees of curvature result from differences in depth of water in the channel in which deposition occurs." This latter situation is illustrated in Figure 67B, in which the individual strata thicken toward the axis of the channel fill.

In another experiment, McKee allowed sediment to settle vertically through a column of quiet water occupying an eroded channel. In this case (Fig. 67C) there is very little thickening of the individual strata toward the axis. Being more or less of equal thickness, the strata tend to restrict the width and depth of the channel progressively as sedimentation proceeds. In a last experiment involving channel fill, McKee caused a submarine current to pass diagonally over the

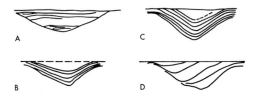

FIG. 67—Tracings of photographs of channel-fill stratification produced in flume experiments. **A.** Trough cross-stratification formed by stream deposition in channel. Surface of water was below channel rims during most of process. **B.** Symmetrically filled channel. Thickening of strata toward bottom of trough. Channel cut by stream and modified by rising water level; filled by submarine current moving down trough. **C.** Symmetrically filled channel. Channel scoured by stream and modified by rising water level. Strata formed by settling from above in quiet water. **D.** Asymmetrically filled channel. Channel cut by stream and modified by rising water level; filled by submarine current moving in direction diagonal to channel. After McKee (1957).

channel, and the result was a very asymmetric channel fill (Fig. 67D). Such asymmetry of the cross-stratification might be expected to develop on the inside of submarine meanders of a stream around growth structures.

In order to relate laboratory flume experiments to natural conditions, several points should be kept in mind. First, practically all channel sandstones (except for those deposited in deltas and around submarine growth structures) are of subaerial deposition. Thus, variations of the situation shown in Figure 67A should apply where cross-stratification is present in a channel fill. Second, the conditions set up to achieve the type of stratification shown in Figure 67C would result in deposition of clay and silt, rather than sand. Only silt and clay could be deposited from suspension in the upper reaches of a *still* body of water occupying an eroded channel, because a velocity of ½–1 knot is necessary to transport sand-size material. Thus, the resulting channel fill would have no commercial significance as a potential reservoir for oil and gas. Third, stratification of the types shown in Figures 67B and 67D will be confined to some deltaic distributaries (but not the bar-finger type of sandstone) and the shallow-water channel sandstones deposited around submarine growth structures. In both of these situations, the subjacent strata are likely to be clays and silty clays which will compact differentially in response to overburden. Thus, any depositional dip of the channel sandstones is likely to be distorted (flattened out) to the extent that the laterally adjacent shales are compacted by the weight of the overburden.

PALEODRAINAGE MAPPING

Very little published material is available on methods of identifying and tracing channel deposits in the subsurface. One paper (Andresen, 1962), however, is particularly worthy to note and review. Andresen presented four methods of locating and tracing trends of valley axes—all of which are based on the depth a valley extends into the subjacent strata. A fifth method involves a determination of the thickness of the valley fill. Although Andresen set up his techniques on a theoretical basis, the writer can vouch for their validity by virtue of having employed strikingly similar, if not the same, techniques for many years in sub-surface studies.

Unconformity-Contour Method

Use of the unconformity-contour method requires that there be a recognizable lithologic distinction between the base of the channel fill and the subjacent strata. The elevation of the base of the channel fill is ascertained from either mechanical or sample logs, or from core data, and a structure map is drawn from these control points (Fig. 68). Axial lines are drawn through the minimum radii of curvature of successive contour lines. Such axial lines exhibit trends of lowest elevation on the unconformity surface.

Andresen (1962) pointed out three possible sources of error in interpretation of the paleodrainage (Fig. 68, A, B, C) by use of this technique. In area A, a northwest-trending syncline is the result of structural deformation after valley carving. This axial trend, being genetically unrelated to erosion, will not contain

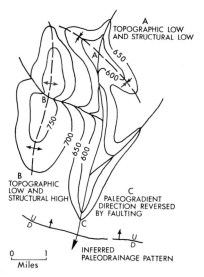

FIG. 68—Valley-structure method for interpreting paleodrainage. After Andresen (1962). Contours in feet.

valley fill. In area B, the topographically low area is elevated where a north-south-trending anticline was superimposed after valley carving. Topographic contour lines normally trend upstream, cross over abruptly, and then trend downstream on the opposite side. This situation has been reversed in the headwaters portion of the stream (west of the anticlinal axis). In area C, faulting has produced an apparent reversal of the paleogradient. Because of these possible sources of error, Andresen recommended that this method be employed only where structural activity has been negligible since the time of valley formation. The writer finds that these structural effects can be anticipated readily and, therefore, need not introduce errors in interpretation. By drawing a structural map on a marker bed a short distance either above or below the valley fill, one can anticipate the modifying effects of tectonic activity and make the proper allowance in reconstructing the paleodrainage (with its valley fill).

Superimposed structural effects can be eliminated almost entirely by constructing an isopach map of the rock section above the lowest point on the marker bed within the area of investigation. A transparency of this map, when superimposed on a map such as that shown in Figure 68, furnishes the necessary data for restoring the surface to a close approximation of its original topographic configuration. At all points of intersection of contour lines of the two maps, new (unconformity) numerical values are established by either adding to or subtracting from (depending on whether the reference datum is above or below the valley fill) the unconformity elevation the thickness of the isopached interval. A contour map of this new set of data will simulate the paleotopography of the unconformity only if the strata were essentially horizontal at the time of valley carving. If marker beds above and below the unconformity are essentially parallel, then it can be assumed that the strata were horizontal at the time of valley carving.

Cross-Section Method

This technique, which is not new, involves the drawing of restricted stratigraphic cross sections by tracing electric or radioactivity logs of wells drilled on subsurface trends of channel fills. To plot a paleodrainage map, lines are drawn which connect the lowest point on each cross section with those on the other cross sections. Such lines will pass through progressively lower points in the direction of the paleogradient. Although Andresen (1962) did not illustrate this method, he pointed out its principal advantages: textures and lithologic types of valley fill can be plotted on the cross sections, and the manner in which the channel migrated across the valley can be observed readily. Andresen noted that it is a time-consuming method and that an advance knowledge of the valley trends is necessary for the proper selection of wells to be used. It is the writer's opinion that the principal value of such a map is to illustrate to management the ideas regarding paleodrainage that are gained by use of the other techniques reviewed here.

Paleogeologic-Map Method

The paleogeologic-map method involves the construction of a subcrop (or

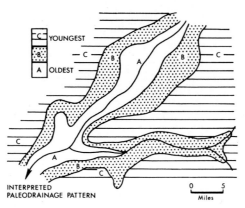

YOUNGEST

OLDEST

INTERPRETED
PALEODRAINAGE PATTERN

0   5
Miles

Fig. 69—Paleogeologic-map method for interpreting paleodrainage. After Andresen (1962).

paleogeologic) map of an unconformity into which a drainage system has been eroded and later filled. In Figure 69, three formations (A, B, and C) have been partly eroded, and their respective subcrop distributions are shown. Valley axes are drawn in the middle parts of the subcrops of the oldest strata. This technique has several limitations. For example, considerable subjectivity is involved in the establishment of formation boundaries; furthermore, downcutting must have been sufficient to expose more than one identifiable stratum. In the northern part of the area shown in Figure 69, the width of the valley exceeds 10 mi (16.0 km). The position of the valley axis is drawn in the middle of subcrop formation A. It is quite likely that a stream flowing in such a broad valley had pronounced meanders within a meander belt which was much less than 10 mi (16.0 km) wide. Thus, the position of the valley axis as generalized might be quite different from the last position of the stream that carved this channel.

The principal application of this method is to sedimentary units deposited in a shelf environment. In this environment, eustatic changes in sea level cause extensive marine transgressions and regressions; as a result, vertical changes in lithology and thinner stratigraphic units are most numerous there. During a regressive phase, conditions are ideal for weathering and selective erosion of thin beds in such an environment. During a readvance of the sea, the base level of deposition of the individual drainage systems retreats landward, and coarser clastic material becomes concentrated in these paleodrainage courses. Because offshelf environments of deposition seldom are exposed to weathering and erosion, unconformities are unlikely to develop; also, the steady conditions of sedimentation cause thicker stratigraphic units to be deposited. It is for these reasons that this technique has almost no application to sedimentary units deposited in offshelf environments.

Marker-Bed Method

The marker-bed method, as illustrated in Figure 70, involves the construction of a modified paleogeologic map. The key to reconstructing paleodrainage is to map areas where a prominent lithologic marker bed is absent owing to valley

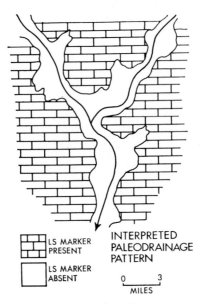

LS MARKER PRESENT

LS MARKER ABSENT

INTERPRETED PALEODRAINAGE PATTERN

0   3
MILES

FIG. 70—Marker-bed method for interpreting paleodrainage. After Andresen (1962).

downcutting. Channel axes then are drawn through the middle of areas where the marker bed has been eroded away. Inasmuch as valleys commonly are asymmetrical in cross section, the paleodrainage pattern is very generalized. Advantages of this technique are that it is easy and rapid. Accuracy in tracing the boundaries of the marker bed is related directly to the amount of available subsurface control. This technique is principally applicable to sediments deposited in the shelf environment, for the same reasons as cited for the paleogeologic-map method.

Datum-Plane–Valley-Floor Isopach Method

This method involves the construction of an isopach map of a stratigraphic interval between the base of valley-fill material and a lithologic marker bed either above or below. Figure 71 illustrates an isopach map of a stratigraphic interval below the base of the channel fill. The minimum interval thickness is directly below the position of maximum downcutting of the stream that carved the channel. Such a map is very similar to a paleotopographic map. The paleogradient may be determined by dividing 5,280 ft by the number of feet of convergence along any 1-mi segment of an axial line.

The mapping of interval L is of limited value where the channel fill contains hydrocarbons. In such a case, a 15–30-ft (4.6–9.1 m) "pocket" generally is drilled below the fill, and most of the producing wells fail to penetrate the lower datum. In tracing the reservoir facies that commonly make up the channel fill, a technique is needed which utilizes the maximum number of control points. The isopach contouring of interval U is such a technique. Interval U is actually a genetic increment of strata, whereas interval L is not. Trends of maximum

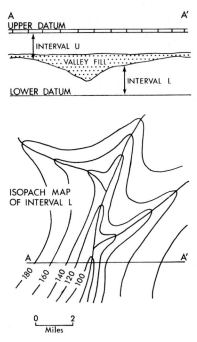

Fɪɢ. 71—Isopach method for interpreting paleodrainage. After Andresen (1962). Contours in feet.

thickness of this GIS are coincident with trends of maximum downcutting. The rate of thickening along axial lines, in feet per mile, is the approximate paleo-gradient.

The advantages of this method are twofold: it uses the maximum number of control points, and it eliminates the problem of selecting a consistent top for the channel fill. In many places the top of a channel fill is transitional with the overlying shales or consists of interbedded thin sandstones and shales. In an isopach map of either interval U or interval L, the effects of tectonism that occurred after deposition of the upper datum are removed and the strata are restored approximately to their original depositional attitude. The emphasis is solely one of reconstructing paleodrainage. This type of map then serves as a geologic framework for reconstructing the geometry of the channel fill. Once the latter has been done, a structure map of either the lower or upper datum should be drawn for the purpose of determining the extent to which "post–upper datum" tectonism may have localized hydrocarbons in structurally high parts of the channel fill.

Valley-Fill Isopach Method

The construction of an isopach map of a channel fill generally is predicated on the assumption that most, if not all, of the fill is sandstone. In such cases, the maximum sandstone trends coincide with trends of maximum downcutting. Unfortunately, most channel fills are a mixture of conglomerate, sandstone, siltstone, and shale. In fact, almost any combination of clastic sedimentary types is possible in a channel fill. Limestone, scattered thin streaks and fragments of coal, and fragments of igneous and metamorphic rocks may constitute parts of a channel fill. If the fill is shale lying on a shale base, it is practically impossible to identify from mechanical logs alone. If it is shale lying on eroded limestone, the contrast is striking on electric and radioactivity logs. The fill commonly consists of lenticular sandstones alternating with shale and siltstone. Several separate oil-reservoir sandstones may be present within a single channel fill, complicating the problem of tracing them in the subsurface.

An isopach map of a channel sandstone does not necessarily reveal the trend and position of maximum downcutting of the stream which carved the channel. Figure 72 shows the thickest part of the sand in a position which does not

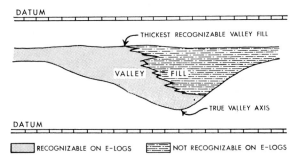

Fig. 72—Thickest sand development versus true valley-axis position. After Andresen (1962).

coincide with that of the true valley axis. Andresen (1962) pointed out that the silty-shale portion of the fill may not be recognizable on electric logs. This problem generally is not as serious as he believed, because a silty shale generally. exhibits a 15–20-mv "shoulder effect" beyond the shale baseline on electric logs. In such instances the base of the channel fill can be ascertained even though the lithology is not that of a reservoir facies.

The principal value of drawing an isopach map of a sandstone such as that illustrated in Figure 72 is one of making reserve estimates. Such a map does not reveal sandstone geometry and is of considerably less value in exploration and stepout drilling than the other types of maps discussed in the preceding paragraphs.

Ancient Examples of Channel Fill

Figure 73 is a structural map of a thin, persistent limestone marker bed, drawn with a contour interval of 20 ft (6.1 m). It shows a southwest homoclinal dip and affords no structural explanation for oil accumulation in pools X and Y. These pools produce oil from different sandstone lenses a short distance below this marker bed. This map was drawn shortly after the completion of a discovery well in pool Y, which had a natural production of 60 bbl of oil per hour from sandstone B of Figure 74. Sandstone A is the producing

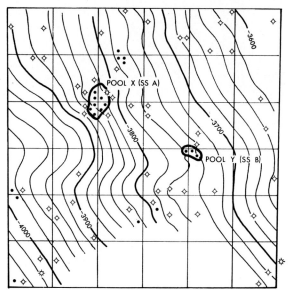

FIG. 73—Structure map of top of limestone 2 (shown on Fig. 74). Contour interval, 20 ft.

formation of pool X of Figure 73. Previous detailed studies of sandstone A, over an area of many townships, revealed that this reservoir is a channel-fill sandstone. In preparing a series of electric-log profiles through these two pools, it is immediately apparent that the predominant shale interval between limestones 1 and 2 thickens and thins abruptly. However, a persistent interval spacing is maintained between limestone 2 and coal and limestone marker beds both above and below limestone 1. Persistent interval thickness (or gradual basinward thickening) is considered a criterion in the selection of a marker-bed reference datum.

Limestone 1 is detrital and blankets an unconformity surface throughout the area of investigation. Although it represents contemporaneity of deposition, the same as limestone 2, it should not be used in selecting the upper limit of a GIS. If limestone 2 is used as the upper reference datum, the top of limestone 1

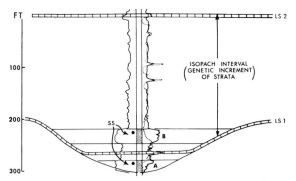

FIG. 74—Diagrammatic channel-fill profile in area of Figure 73.

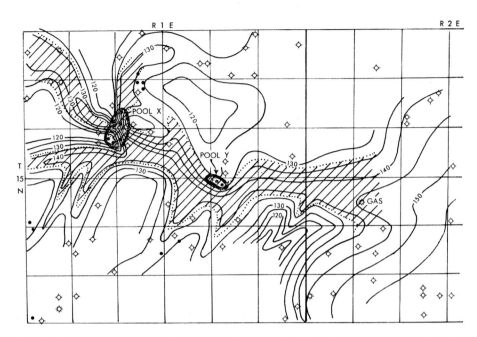

FIG. 75—Genetic-increment map (limestone 1 to limestone 2 of Fig. 74) showing a subdued replica of a paleodrainage course. Diagonally shaded area indicates trend and width of sandstone B of Figure 74. Contours in feet.

will present a subdued replica of the unconformity surface. The lowest part of the unconformity is at the base of sandstone A. The channel fill in Figure 74 is an alternating series of lenticular sandstones, shale, and limestone. Inasmuch as limestone 1 is present in all wells except one (in which sandstone B thickens downward and truncates it), the genetic increment of strata indicated in Figure 74 is an ideal one for reconstructing a subdued replica of the paleotopography of the unconformity.

Figure 75 is an isopach map of the GIS shown in Figure 74. The diagonally shaded area is an estimate of the trend and distribution of sandstone B. Although pool X (Fig. 73) produces from sandstone A, sandstone B also has good reservoir characteristics in these wells; however, it will not be produced until the reserves in sandstone A are depleted.

It can be seen readily that there is no similarity between Figures 73 and 75. Only when a sandstone-distribution map (shaded area, Fig. 75) is drawn should structural considerations be made. An isolated gas well 3 mi (4.8 km) east of pool Y had an initial production of 10 million cu ft of gas from sandstone B, but is shut in for lack of a pipeline connection to the market. This zone is approximately 150 ft (46 m) higher structurally in this well than the oil-producing zone of pool Y. Subsequent development drilling within the shaded area between pools X and Y has merged these two pools into one.

A good example of an oil-reservoir sandstone of a channel-fill type is illustrated in Figure 76. The stratigraphic profile, *A-A'*, of the channel fill and

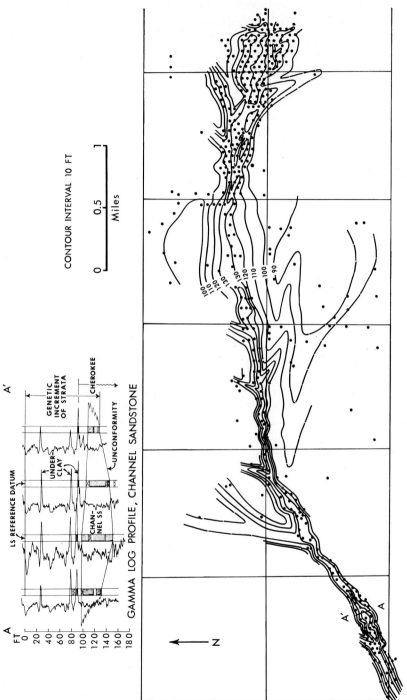

Fig. 76—Isopach map of genetic increment of strata which includes an oil-saturated channel sandstone. Mapped interval is shown on inserted gamma-log profile *A-A'*. After Busch (1963).

overlying strata is constructed from gamma logs supplemented by cores. The sandstone thickens primarily at the expense of the underlying shale. The reference datum at the top of the profile is a limestone marker bed representing contemporaneity of deposition. It can be identified readily on all gamma logs and also was reliably logged by the drillers in those wells which were not mechanically logged. Thus, this limestone serves as a very useful reference datum not only over all of the 11-sq mi (28.5 sq km) area illustrated, but also over the surrounding area. The stratigraphic interval between this reference datum and the base of the channel sandstone contains no disconformities and, therefore, constitutes a genetic increment of strata. A close inspection of the isopach map of this interval reveals that the interval increases in thickness from east to west; the increase is approximately 60 ft (18.3 m) in a distance of about 6 mi (9.7 km). The average paleogradient is about 10 ft/mi (1.9 m/km); the direction of stream flow was to the west. The channel fill is predominantly sandstone which is interrupted locally with shale and siltstone and scarce limestone "breaks." The sandstone is in sharp contact with shale both to the north and south; this is a true cut-and-fill channel.

This isopach map may be visualized in the same manner as a topographic map of a modern stream channel. The contour lines extend for considerable distances upstream, cross the channel abruptly, and then extend downstream on the opposite side. Thus, this map represents a topographic simulation of a stream channel in which a more or less continuous lenticular body of sandstone was deposited. The filling of the channel probably was effected by an upstream shift of the base level of deposition of the stream when the area was inundated by a west-to-east marine transgression.

Detailed stratigraphic studies of this area, and of the surrounding area, indicate that this channel was carved in a region of comparatively low topographic relief. The channel was cut into uniformly nonresistant, partially consolidated muds. Essential parallelism of thin limestones and coal marker beds present in the shales both above and below the channel fill indicates a horizontal attitude of the beds at the time of channel carving. Thus, any drainage pattern developed on such a land surface should be dendritic. The ancient stream channel illustrated in Figure 76 represents only one of a series of such channels that must constitute a dendritic drainage system. Furthermore, any tributaries, regardless of whether they are primary, secondary, or tertiary, are likely to join their respective master streams at an acute angle. To locate another channel fill of the dendritic network of which this channel appears to be a component part, it is necessary to know the original direction of stream flow. Any possible tributaries will bear an acute angular relationship to this ancient stream course.

To locate the most likely positions of tributary-stream "breakouts," it is important to examine closely the cores, logs, and productivity of all wells along the margin of this lenticular channel sandstone. An apparently localized or abrupt increase in sandstone thickness, or an anomalously large cumulative

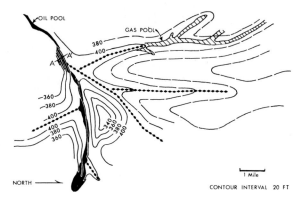

Fig. 77—Isopach map of Cherokee Group (Lower Pennsylvanian) showing oil and gas pools in an upper Cherokee sandstone. Trends of these elongate pools are coincident with narrow trends of thicker Cherokee Group. Patterned lines also indicate axial trends of thicker Cherokee. After Busch (1963).

production of a well along the margin, might signal the site of a tributary "breakout."

Figure 77 is an isopach map of a genetic sequence of strata in which the oil-producing channel sandstone is present. It includes not only the area illustrated in Figure 76, but also additional territory to the north. The east-west-trending pool, shown in black, is the same one that occupies the sandstone-filled channel of Figure 76.

The stratigraphic relation of the oil-bearing sandstone to the genetic increment of strata of Figure 76, and to the genetic sequence of strata of Figure 77, is illustrated in Figure 78. The presence of an unconformity at the base of the GSS was determined by constructing numerous stratigraphic profiles in the area illustrated in Figure 77. Abrupt changes in interval thickness below the lowest coal bed clearly indicate that the topographic lows of the unconformity surface were filled with sediment before marine deposition occurred on the topographic highs. After these hills were obliterated by filling of the intervening low areas, an alternating series of as many as eight coal beds was formed during the time represented by the GSS. This repetitious sequence indicates the following conditions: a monotonous mud-flat environment in which there was a cover of extensive vegetation, followed by minor subsidence and clastic deposition, and then repetitions of this series of conditions.

The oil pool of Figure 77, for the most part, coincides with the trend and position of a linear area where the GSS has a maximum thickness. Furthermore, a lenticular gas-bearing sandstone is present along the west margin of the northern half of this area. This lenticular sandstone is stratigraphically equivalent to the sandstone that produces oil in a cross-trend to the south. This gas-bearing sandstone is also in a linear belt of maximum thickness of the GSS. This relation of oil- and gas-bearing sandstone to maximum GSS thickness is more than a coincidence. Thin areas of the GSS coincide with paleo-

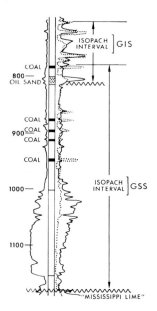

FIG. 78—Electric-log section of Lower Pennsylvanian showing relation of stratigraphic intervals mapped in Figures 76 and 77. After Busch (1963).

topographic highs on the underlying unconformity, and, conversely, thick areas (or trends) represent paleotopographic lows on this surface. Areas where the GSS is thicker have undergone slightly more compaction than nearby areas where it is thinner. Thus, it is postulated that slight topographic depressions developed in the mud flats toward the end of deposition of the GSS as a result of differential compaction of a predominantly shale section over buried hills. These depressions served as focal points for surface runoff of meteoric water; thus, erosion was initiated. Runoff over uniformly nonresistant, essentially horizontal strata resulted in a dendritic drainage pattern.

Several divergent thick trends of the GSS of Figure 77 are indicated by patterned lines. It is along these lines that additional channel sandstones might be found. These trends, together with the known trends of two oil- and gas-bearing channel sandstones, make up the complete dendrite of the drainage pattern which is likely to have developed late in the period of GSS deposition.

Submarine-Canyon Fill, Lavaca County, Texas

The middle Wilcox of the central Gulf Coast of Texas affords an excellent example of a very large channel filled largely with silty shale. The shale fill is in a canyon incised into a very thick sandy section of typical Wilcox strata. An isopach map of the channel fill is shown in Figure 79. Hoyt (1959, p. 41) stated: "At its maximum known development near the town of Yoakum it has a width of 10 miles and a depth of 3,000 feet." It has been traced upstream, to the northwest, for approximately 50 mi (80.5 km). Hoyt postulated that this channel resulted from slumps and slides on the face of the steep, unstable mass of thick sediments

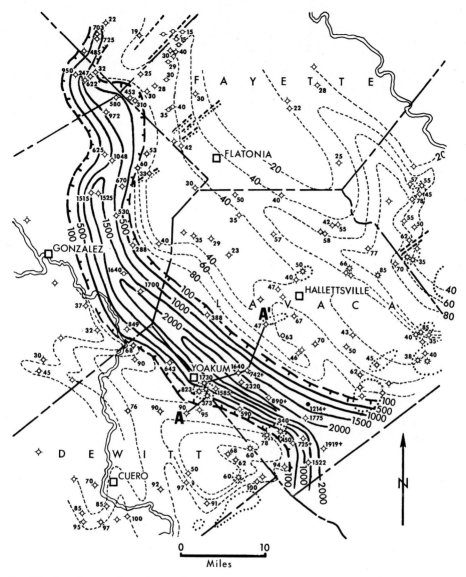

Fig. 79—Isopach map of a middle Wilcox channel fill in central Gulf Coast of Texas. Solid contour lines are after Hoyt (1959); contour interval, 500 ft. Dashed contour lines were added by the writer from data furnished by Hoyt; contour interval, 20 ft.

deposited out to the edge of an Eocene shelf. He considered faulting to have been the triggering mechanism which ". . . set up turbidity currents as the bottom of the gorge was reached." Waters of the stream would provide the fluidity and mobility that would be necessary in order for the current to erode and deepen the channel.

Figure 80, which is a cross section of the channel fill, clearly illustrates its

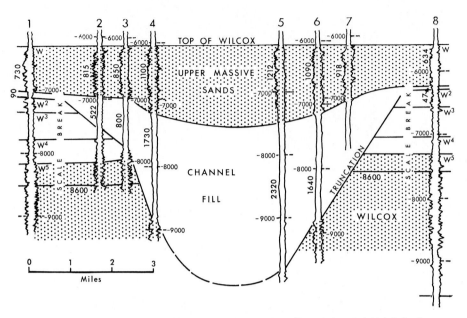

FIG. 80—Log-section, middle Wilcox channel. Location of profile (*A-A'* = left-right) is shown on Figure 79. After Hoyt (1959).

silty-shale character. Bedded Wilcox sandstone borders the channel on both sides and massive sandstones are present above the channel fill. Hoyt (1959) noted that

> . . . the base of the upper massive sands of the Wilcox rests directly upon the shale of the channel fill and also upon the blanket stratum of shale. This and the fact that the channel shale thins progressively to both the east and the west rims of the channel to connect with the comparatively thin stratum of shale should be sufficient indication that the time of deposition of the shale fill was contemporaneous with the deposition of the blanket shale stratum.

Hoyt made no effort to contour the thickness of this shale blanket beyond the confines of the channel, where it is less than 100 ft (30.5 m) thick (Fig. 79). The dashed contour lines on either side of the main channel are the writer's interpretation of the thickness data furnished by Hoyt. From this additional contouring it is apparent that several other silty-shale-filled channels are present northeast and southwest of the main channel, though they are much less pronounced.

The upper massive sandstone (Fig. 80) is 500 ft (152 m) or more thicker in the central channel than at the edges. This is an example of compensatory deposition of a thicker sand as a result of differential compaction of the underlying thick shale body.

The Yoakum gas pool is situated 2 mi (3.2 km) southeast of the city of Yoakum. Production is from nine wells drilled into the 8,600-ft (2,620 m) sandstone (Fig. 81). Accumulation is in a west-southwest-plunging structural

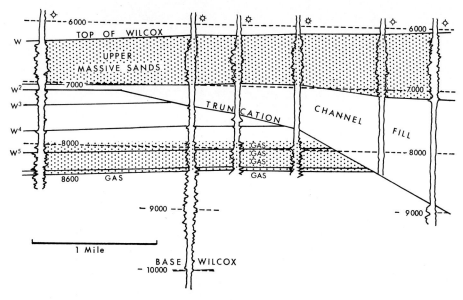

Fig. 81—Structural profile through Yoakum gas pool, showing continuity of sandstone to point of truncation by silty-shale wedge of channel fill. After Hoyt (1959).

nose. The updip limit of accumulation is abruptly defined by truncation of the bedded Wilcox reservoir sandstone. The western wedge edge of the channel fill has prevented further updip migration of the gas.

Figure 82 is a structure map of the base of the blanket shale and the base of the shale fill of the channel. The 500-ft (152 m) contour interval is too great to reveal the much less significant channels mapped on either side of the main channel (Fig. 79). Hoyt (1959) pointed out that, "A connection of the −7000 foot contour from the west rim to the east rim of the channel would pass at right angles over the −10,000 foot contour of the channel floor, indicating that the channel was 3,000 feet deep at this point." By subtracting the original depth of the channel at this point from the present depth, it is apparent that about 7,000 ft (2,130 m) of basinward tilt has occurred since deposition of the Wilcox strata.

In an effort to explain this conspicuous channel fill, Hoyt postulated an abrupt and extensive marine transgression that resulted in rapid filling of the gorge with silty shale and the deposition of a thin blanket of shale over the area on either side of the deep channel. Marine regression then resulted in deposition of thick, extensive sands as a blanket. As pointed out, there was compensatory thickening of the regressive, upper massive sands over the compacted shales of the channel fill.

Cyclic Muddy Sandstones, Northeastern Wyoming

The Muddy Sandstone Member of the Thermopolis Shale of northeastern Wyoming consists of a series of very lenticular sandstone bodies. The Muddy is

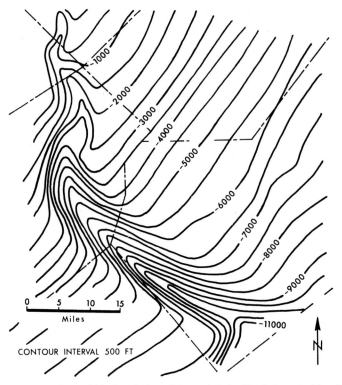

Fig. 82—Structure map, base of blanket shale and base of shale fill of channel. After Hoyt (1959).

in the upper part of the Lower Cretaceous. The Muddy is overlain conformably by the Mowry Shale; it unconformably overlies irregularly eroded portions of the Skull Creek Shale. This zone of sandstone lenses has been studied in a 576-sq mi (1,489 km²) area which includes all of Townships 47–54N and Ranges 67–70W, encompassing contiguous parts of Weston, Crook, and Campbell Counties.

Easily identified siltstone and bentonite marker beds above and below the Muddy sandstones facilitate identification and correlation of the individual sandstone members composing the Muddy zone. Figure 83 is a stratigraphic cross section which illustrates a bentonite marker bed (reference datum) in the Mowry Shale, above the Muddy sandstones, and two siltstone zones in the Skull Creek Shale, below the Muddy. The position of the unconformity at the base of the lowest development of Muddy sandstone is clearly indicated. The stratigraphically lowest units of the Muddy Sandstone Member occur where erosion into the underlying Skull Creek Shale was deepest. The several sandstone units are designated alphabetically from the base up, in the order of deposition.

Figure 84 is a stratigraphic profile of an area 7–10 mi (11.3–16.0 km) south of that of Figure 83. The sandstone units of the Muddy zone are lenticular. The "C" sandstone is the lowest unit present on Figure 84, whereas the "AA" member is the lowest unit present farther north (Fig. 83). Thus, the maximum downcutting at the unconformity increased from south to north. The maximum down-

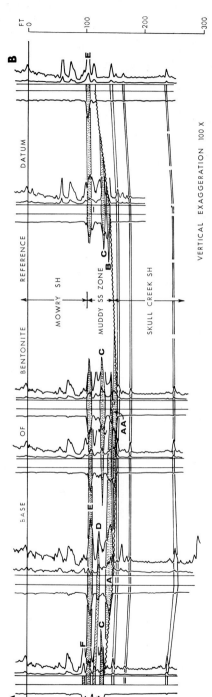

FIG. 83—Stratigraphic profile *A-B*. Reference datum is base of a bentonite marker bed. This illustration shows lenticular nature of sandstone members composing Muddy zone, as well as downcutting of unconformity surface into Skull Creek Shale. Location of profile is shown on Figure 85.

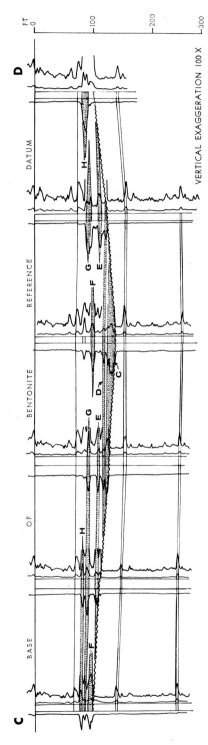

FIG. 84—Stratigraphic profile *C-D*. Reference datum is base of a bentonite marker bed. Sandstone members of Muddy zone present along axial trend of unconformity surface are stratigraphically higher than in Figure 83. Location of profile is shown on Figure 85.

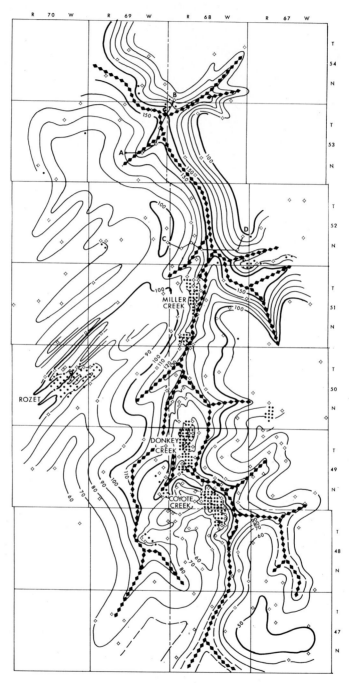

FIG. 85—Isopach map of genetic increment of strata between bentonite marker bed and unconformity at base of Muddy sandstone zone. Map shows simulated paleotopographic surface of unconformity before deposition of Muddy sandstone. Contour interval, 10 ft.

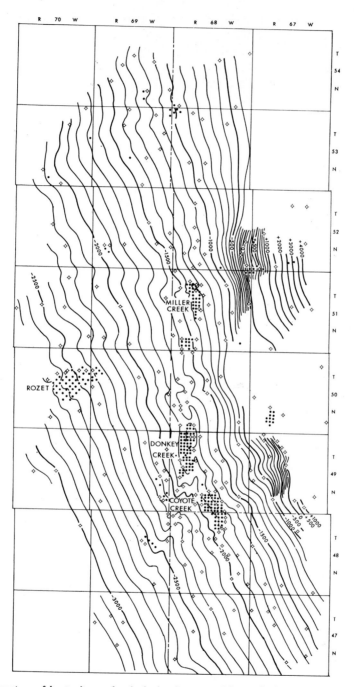

FIG. 86—Structure of bentonite marker bed, showing general homoclinal westward tilt into Powder River basin. Contour intervals, 100 ft and 500 ft.

cutting can be determined readily by preparing an isopach map of the genetic increment of strata between the bentonite reference datum and the unconformity. Figure 85 is such a map. It clearly shows a north-flowing drainage system which was eroded into the soft shales of the Skull Creek.

The Miller Creek, Donkey Creek, and Coyote Creek oil pools all produce principally from the stratigraphically lower Fall River sandstones. There is an abrupt sandstone-to-shale facies change along the eastern margins of all these pools. Approximately 200 ft (61 m) of Skull Creek Shale separates the Fall River sandstones from the higher Muddy sandstones. It is postulated that differential compaction of the Skull Creek directly east of the Miller Creek, Donkey Creek, and Coyote Creek pools was a determinative factor in the location of the main axial trend of this Muddy sandstone drainage course.

The structure of the bentonite marker bed is shown in Figure 86. There is slightly more than 6,500 ft (1,980 m) of basinward (Powder River basin) homoclinal dip to the west; a localized closure is present over the Donkey Creek oil pool. All of this westward tilting is related to the post-Cretaceous Laramide orogeny.

The combination of paleotopographic map (Fig. 85) and structure map (Fig. 86) serves as a geologic framework for more detailed studies of the oil possibilities of the sandstone units of the Muddy. The trends and geographic distribution of each of these sandstones can be determined readily by (1) identifying each of the alphabetical sandstone units in each well, and (2) outlining each of the sandstones on an acetate overlay by following the contour lines of the paleotopography (Fig. 85). Because there are nine sandstone units of the Muddy in this area, there is

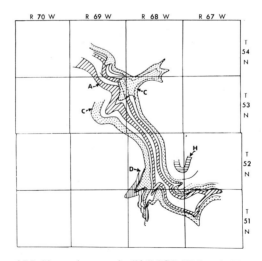

FIG. 87—Distribution of Muddy sandstone units "A," "C," "D," and "H." Units "A" and "C" are shown as paired bands on opposite sides of principal paleodrainage courses. Stratigraphically higher sandstone units are progressively more widely separated and cross over main stream axes successively farther upstream.

considerable overlap. Thus, several acetate overlay maps must be drawn to avoid confusion. One such sandstone-distribution map is illustrated in Figure 87. It shows the respective distributions of sandstones "A," "C," "D," and "H." Sandstones "A" and "C" appear as narrow bands on either side of the axes of the main channel and its tributaries. By following any one band of sandstone in an upstream direction, it will be noted that it crosses the axis and extends downstream on the opposite side. Furthermore, the two bands of any one sandstone are farther from the channel axis the higher they are in the section. Thus, in profile, they have an *en échelon* arrangement on opposite sides of the channel. This pairing of sandstone bands on opposite sides of the channel is interpreted as the result of cyclic subsidence and marine transgression, which moved from north to south. By this postulation, each pair of sandstone bands is the result of a stillstand of the shoreline during which fringing beach sands were deposited.

To define drillable prospects in such sinuous bands of lenticular sandstones, it is necessary to use a combination of sandstone distribution (Fig. 87) and structural configuration (Fig. 86). Only the updip wedge edges of the individual sandstone members are likely to afford favorable conditions for the entrapment of oil and gas. No two pools are likely to have the same outline, and each of the sandstone members must be considered as a separate potential source of supply.

7

deltas

INTRODUCTION

Only within the past 15–20 years have petroleum explorationists really begun to recognize the economic significance of deltas. With this recognition has come a realization of the variabilities of deltas—both external and internal. For decades, little more was known about ancient deltas than that which was published by Barrell (1914) on the classic Catskill-Chemung delta of the Appalachian geosyncline and the much smaller deltas of glacial Lake Bonneville described by Gilbert (1885). In more recent years, several significant papers treating ancient deltas have appeared in the literature. Busch (1953) described the Pennsylvanian Booch delta of the Arkoma basin; Nanz (1954) the Oligocene sandstone reservoir of the Seeligson field of the Gulf Coast; Weimer (1961) the Late Cretaceous Rawlins delta; Halbouty and Barber (1961) an Oligocene delta of the Gulf Coast; Rainwater (1963) a Gulf Coast Miocene delta; and Swann (1964) a Late Mississippian Michigan River delta. In reviewing these papers, it becomes apparent that no two of the deltas described are alike and that considerable background relative to modern deltas and their respective depositional environments is an essential prerequisite to their recognition and delineation in the subsurface. Modern deltas have certain distinct differences, too, which are related to such variables as stream gradient, stream density (suspended and dissolved load), relative abundance and type of suspended load, basin-water density, width of the mouth of the effluent stream, shape of the depositional basin, and energy levels within the basin.

In 1951, the American Petroleum Institute initiated Project 51, which lasted for 7 years and consisted of an intensive series of investigations of modern sediments, and their respective environments of deposition, along the northwestern

108

Gulf of Mexico. The depositional environments and sediments of the delta of the Mississippi River were intensively investigated, and numerous papers were published. This work and numerous studies by individuals in more recent years make the sediments of the Mississippi River deltaic plain the most completely understood modern depositional environment anywhere in the world. Undoubtedly many, and possibly most, of the sedimentary processes in operation in this area today have worldwide application in both modern and ancient sediments. Ironically, however, the modern birdfoot delta of the Mississippi River should not be considered as typical of the majority of modern and ancient deltas of the world. As discussed elsewhere, this Holocene delta is the result of a combination of environmental variables that exists in only a very few places in the world today.

THEORY OF JET FLOW

Any river discharging its turbulent fluid into a still body of water such as a lake or ocean may be considered as a free jet. Bates (1953) and Bates and Freeman (1953) have reviewed the nature of jet flow from the writings of aerodynamicists and chemical, heating, and hydraulic engineers, and have made direct applications of their findings to a better understanding of delta formation. In fact, they showed that three distinct types of deltas may be formed within a basin. They note that there are two basic types of jet flow—plane jet, in which mixing occurs in two directions along a horizontal plane, and axial jet, in which mixing is three-dimensional. Bates (1953, p. 2120–2121) wrote that, in the case of

> . . . purely inertial flow, the lateral boundaries of the axial jet continue to spread downstream at a constant angle of about 20°. In plane jet, however, spreading of the lateral boundaries decreases downstream so that a parabolic shape develops in which the width of the jet of turbid water is of the order of three times the square root of the distance downstream from the mouth. Moreover, mixing in all three dimensions permits the axial jet to expend itself in a fraction of the distance required for the plane jet to disappear.

It is known that there can be an appreciable hydraulic head at the mouth of a stream and that such a head results in more rapid spreading and a greater forward velocity than does purely inertial jet flow. The effects of such a hydraulic head are not considered in the basic jet theory, which considers only inertial flow.

Figure 88, taken from Bates (1953, p. 2122), shows the distribution of forward velocity of effluent water as it discharges through a well-defined orifice (mouth of a stream) in plane jet flow. In this diagram,

$$D_y = \text{width of the orifice;}$$
$$X = \text{distance downstream from the orifice;}$$
$$U_0 = \text{centerline velocity at point of issuance; and}$$
$$U = \text{centerline velocity at any point.}$$

That part of the basin extending from 0 to $4D_y$ away from the orifice is referred to as the *zone of flow establishment*. Within the central part of this

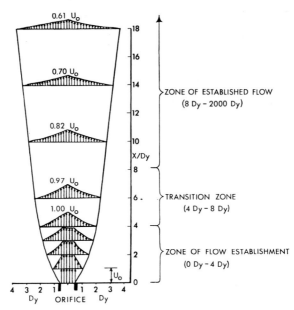

FIG. 88—Distribution of forward velocity in plane jet. After Bates (1953).

zone there is no appreciable deceleration of centerline (orifice) velocity. Along the margins of this zone of flow establishment, however, deceleration causes fine-grained sediment to settle out of suspension to form natural levees. Such levees consist predominantly of silt and clay with some mixture of fine-grained sand. Farther out in the basin, within the area between the two hyperbolic curves, is the *transition zone,* which extends a distance of 4–8D_y from the orifice. Within this distance the constant core velocity changes to a standard rate of deceleration and a cross-trending lunate bar is deposited. This transverse bar consists almost entirely of sand, which grades laterally and near the base into silt and silty clay. The two ends of this bar link with the distal ends of the natural levees that are present on either side of the zone of flow establishment, and thus block the mouth of the stream. With continued discharge of effluent waters and their suspended load, the transverse bar continues to build upward to the level where "breakouts" must occur. Such new outlets will break either through low points on the transverse bar or through the levees, or both. Thus, the distributary system of a river is born.

When the lunate bar develops within the *transition zone,* Bates (1953) pointed out, there is a "major reduction in channel depth," which must be compensated for

> . . . by an over-all increase in channel width at the distributary mouths, so that the cross-sectional area of the stream and consequently the velocity of flow will then remain nearly constant until the river water enters the ocean. However, because of greater water friction, shallow channels are somewhat more inefficient than deep channels of the same cross-sectional area and a small increase in the sum total of

the cross-sectional area of distributary mouths is to be expected over the cross-sectional area of the master channel.

He noted that this principle is supported by the splitting of tributaries of the lower Mississippi River, increasing the ". . . total channel area by not more than 10 percent of the original area, while mean depths of distributaries were only 42–72 percent of the main channel depth."

A third zone within the distribution of forward velocity (Fig. 88) is called the *zone of established flow*. It extends from a distance $8D_y$ from the orifice to more than $2,000D_y$ in the case of plane jet flow. Within this large area, silt- and clay-size material settles out of suspension to form the prodelta clays.

In axial jet flow the mixing of effluent water with water of the embayment is three-dimensional (x, y, and z planes). The position of the transverse bar in such a case is at a distance of 4–$8D_z$ (D_z = diameter of circular orifice) from the orifice, rather than 4–$8D_y$ as with plane jet flow. As practically all rivers are much wider than deep, it is very important to know whether the turbid water of the river behaves as an axial or a plane jet. The transverse bar of an axial jet stream will develop much closer to the orifice than that of a plane jet stream. In axial jet flow there also is a much shorter distance of deceleration within the zone of established flow—*i.e.*, $200D_z$ rather than $2,000D_y$.

Basic Types of Deltas

The types of deltas formed at the mouths of streams are determined largely by the relative densities of the effluent water and the water of the embayment (lake or ocean). If the turbid water of the stream has a density exceeding that of the water of the embayment, it is referred to as *hyperpycnal inflow* (Fig. 89), which is one of the two types of plane jet flow. In such a case the sediment-bearing fluid slides under the water of the embayment and tends to erode a submarine channel along the shelf of the basin and to carve a submarine canyon in the bathyal part of a continental slope. Vertical mixing is minimal. A submarine delta will be deposited just basinward from the point of abrupt decrease in gradient. Such deltas are formed far offshore in deep water as the result of density, or turbidity, currents.

If the effluent water has approximately the same density as the water of the embayment, the term *homopycnal inflow* is used (Fig. 90). The waters mix in three dimensions and the flow pattern is that of an axial jet. The several

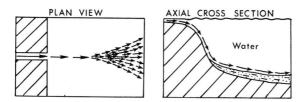

Fig. 89—Submarine delta, hyperpycnal inflow. After Bates and Freeman (1953).

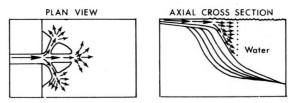

FIG. 90—Gilbert-type delta, homopycnal inflow. After Bates and Freeman (1953).

zones of deceleration are much shorter than with plane jet flow, and a delta with conspicuous topset, foreset, and bottomset beds is formed. In fact, the slope of the foreset beds may be as great as the angle of repose, which is approximately 30°. This type of delta, described by Gilbert (1885), usually is developed along the margins of freshwater lakes where there is very little density contrast between the water of the lake and that of streams flowing into the lake. Most authors of physical geology textbooks have assumed that all deltas are of the Gilbert type, without taking into account the fact that Gilbert described and illustrated deltas of a lacustrine environment rather than a marine environment. As a consequence, many geologists mistakenly look for steeply tilted foreset beds in marine deltas.

A third, and most significant, basic type of delta results from *hypopycnal inflow,* in which the turbulent discharge waters of a stream are less dense than the water of the embayment into which they flow. This is a second type of plane jet flow in which mixing is in only two directions as the effluent water spreads blanketlike over the more dense embayment water (Fig. 91). Practically all rivers flowing into the oceans today are of this type, and such must be postulated for the geologic past. Bates (1953) pointed out that, "If the magnitude of discharge is small, a lunate bar forms off the outlet; if the discharge is moderate to large, a cuspate, arcuate, or bird-foot type of delta will form." In further discussion of the types of deltas likely to develop, he wrote (p. 2155):

The question then arises as to whether this basic pattern of deltaic deposition will

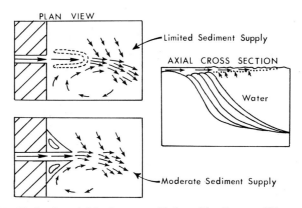

FIG. 91—Marine littoral delta, hypopycnal inflow. After Bates and Freeman (1953).

give rise to a lunate bar, a cuspate delta, or a bird-foot delta with major permanent distributaries. In nature, the deltaic shape which finally develops depends on the magnitude of the non-equilibrium existing between the coastal forces of accretion and erosion operating near the outlet. For example, rough computations made for coastal conditions between the Mississippi River delta and Freeport, Texas, indicate that streams with average annual discharges less than 500 cubic feet per second through natural channels do not introduce enough sediment into the sea to counterbalance the rate at which coastal material is being moved seaward by wave action. Streams with average annual discharges of 500–8,000 cubic feet per second are able to develop active lunate bars off their mouth, while annual discharges of the order of 15,000 cubic feet per second are adequate to develop permanent cuspate deltas. Average annual discharges of more than 50,000 cubic feet per second through channels without settling basins are required for natural levee systems that build seaward despite wave action to make up key parts of the bird-foot delta.

Although the relations between these variable rates of volumetric discharge and the types of deltas formed appear significant, data are insufficient to warrant generalizations. The rate of discharge can be considered only one of several significant variables bearing on the type of delta likely to form. No two rivers have the same balance between the forces of erosion and accretion at their mouths. Waves, longshore currents, tides, and even Coriolis force, individually and collectively, have a direct bearing on the type of delta to be formed. Other controlling factors include surface slope of the inflow, river gradient, basin slope, amount and type of suspended load, water temperatures, and even eustatic changes in sea level. With the exception of quantity and type of suspended load, most of these factors appear to be of lesser modifying significance than the rate of volumetric discharge.

CLASSIFICATION OF DELTAS

Despite the numerous factors that bear on the types of deltas likely to form, there appear to be a finite number of shapes that can be recognized readily in modern and ancient sediments. In Bates' (1953) three basic types, the prime emphasis is on the relative densities of the river water and the water of the embayment. These are environmental factors of prime importance. Deltas theoretically could be classified on the basis of environmental factors, internal lithologic characteristics, relative number and nature of distributaries, or shape. Any classification based on environmental factors or number and nature of distributaries would have little application when considering ancient deltas. Even a classification based on internal parameters would have only limited application because of our incomplete knowledge. It is the writer's opinion that a preliminary classification based on shape is all that is justifiable until diagnostic criteria of an environmental and lithologic nature have been clearly demonstrated and cataloged. At any rate, ancient deltas are known whose distinctive shapes seem to have counterparts in modern depositional environments. Undoubtedly, a better understanding of deltas later will lead to the establishment of subtypes and to a more complete classification.

Arcuate Delta

Herodotus, 2,500 years ago, recognized the similarity in shape of the sub-aerial part of the Nile delta and the Greek letter (Δ); thus, he referred to this large accretionary area as a delta. A closer inspection of the shape (Fig. 92A) reveals a three-sided outline with the shoreward margin convex (or arcuate) in a seaward direction. The delta of the Nile River generally is considered the prototype of all deltas.

Estuarine Delta

The estuarine delta is funnel-shaped and has a length generally several times greater than its maximum width, as illustrated by the Mackenzie River delta (Fig. 92B). The distributaries are braided and anastomosing, and are separated by sandbars or islands, which locally may be silty. The composition of this sediment is controlled almost entirely by the nature of the weathered rock material transported by the river. Estuarine sediments may accumulate in certain river mouths where the direction of stream flow is reversed by daily tidal incursions. Estuaries occur in river mouths along shorelines of submergence. Estuarine deltas, however, do not accumulate in all estuaries. They form only in those in which the opposing forces of stream and tidal energies are nearly equal and where the streams are transporting sand- and silt-size sediment in addition to clay-size material. Nanz (1954) described an excellent example of an ancient (Oligocene) delta.

Birdfoot Delta

This type of delta, as the name implies, has the shape of a bird's foot (Fig. 92C). The distributaries are relatively few in number and the width of the individual channels is great compared to their depth. Such deltas are built into deeper waters than are the more common arcuate type—either near the edge of a continental shelf or in a lacustrine environment where there is a comparatively abrupt "drop off" at the mouth of a stream draining into a lake. This type of delta is not common, although conspicuous examples of marginal-marine and lacustrine birdfoot deltas can be cited for the Mississippi and St. Clair Rivers, respectively. A brief review of the modern Mississippi River delta is presented in the discussion of modern deltas. Similar information is not available for the St. Clair River delta.

Lobate Delta

The term "lobate delta" is proposed here for those river-derived sediments which have an attenuated distribution in a basinward direction. Bates (1953, p. 2128–2129) discussed one such delta formed by the ancestral Mississippi River during Pleistocene time (Fig. 92D) under hyperpycnal-inflow conditions. Fisk (1944) pointed out that sea level was as much as 450 ft (137 m) lower than at present at five separate times. During these stages of lower sea level, the ancestral Mississippi River eroded a canyon across the subaerially exposed

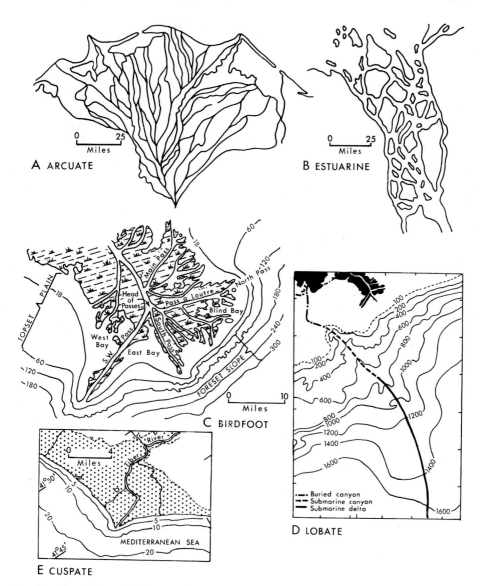

FIG. 92—Classification of deltas by shape. **A.** Arcuate delta. **B.** Estuarine delta. **C.** Birdfoot delta. **D.** Lobate delta. **E.** Cuspate delta.

shelf of the Gulf of Mexico. Fisk (1952) stated that the head of the canyon was about at the mouth of the Mississippi River during the late Wisconsin low stand of sea level. Bates (1953) commented that,

> About 1,200 cubic miles of clastic sediment having been eroded out of the Mississippi alluvial valley during each lowering of sea-level, it becomes evident that if the eroded material of one or two glacial stages moved seaward over the same path as a series of turbidity flows the canyon development attributed to the Pleistocene

could well have occurred. Moreover, the basinward movement of this sediment should have built a delta at the mouth of the canyon.

A possible indication of this submarine delta is the pronounced bulge of the water-depth contours of Figure 92D in the area off the canyon's mouth between 700 and 1,700 fm. If the seaward slope of this portion of the seafloor were restored to its Pleistocene slope, this lobate delta would be narrower and more attenuated.

Another example of a lobate delta is that described by Pepper *et al.* (1954, Pl. 182; see Fig. 92D). This Early Mississippian delta probably was formed in a shallow epeiric sea. It consists predominantly of red shales into which were incised deep channels that subsequently were filled with sands. The main channel did not split into a series of distributaries near its mouth, as with an arcuate delta; rather, it fed numerous side channels which split off at various points along its course. This delta undoubtedly was deposited under strikingly different environmental conditions than that of the ancestral Mississippi River. Dunbar and Rodgers (1957) postulated that it was formed in a shallow epeiric sea in which tides probably were negligible. They stated (p. 88),

> With the Cincinnati Arch forming a long peninsula, Cincinnatia, on the west, the Ohio Bay must have lacked great storm waves so that the rivers were completely dominant over marine forces. Nevertheless, the bay was so shallow that locally produced waves could reach bottom everywhere helping to spread the fine sediment. No break in slope can be detected, and the entire complex apparently consists of topset beds.

Cuspate Delta

A cuspate delta is one in which triangle-shaped deposits accumulate on either side of the main channel as it accretes seaward from the original shoreline. This type of delta presents a striking contrast to the arcuate delta in that it converges basinward almost to a point. Furthermore, it is split down the middle by a single channel without any significant distributaries. Bates (1953) attributed this type of delta to those river mouths where the annual volumetric discharge is of the order of 15,000 cu ft/second (420 m^3/second), and he cited the Brazos River delta, Texas, as an example. Another example is the delta of the Tiber (Tevere) River, Italy, illustrated in Figure 92E.

Mississippi River Delta

The delta of the Mississippi River represents only the most recent deposit of a river which has formed no less than six deltas, which collectively are called a "deltaic plain." Geologic literature treating both this modern birdfoot delta and the deltaic plain to which it is related is abundant and complete. For a complete review of the various facies, their environments of deposition, and the general history of the deltaic plain, the reader is referred to Trowbridge (1930), Russell (1936), Russell and Russell (1939), Fisk (1944), Fisk *et al.* (1954), Scruton (1960), and Kolb and Van Lopik (1966). In this review of the Mississippi River deltaic complex, emphasis is placed primarily on those aspects which, in the writer's opinion, appear to have the most significance in recognizing and analyzing its counterparts in the subsurface.

The modern birdfoot (Balize) delta of the Mississippi River has formed in a little less than 500 years. The subaerial portion of this delta is about 131 sq mi (339 km²) in area. More than three fourths of the sediment, however, extends below sea level, where it is deposited on a broad platform out to an approximate water depth of 300 ft (91 m; see Fig. 92C). Thus, the combined area of the subaerial and submarine parts of this delta is about 700 sq mi (1,783 km²). This size is in sharp contrast to that of earlier deltas of the Mississippi, which range up to 3,000 sq mi (7,770 km²) in area. The maximum thickness, including the prodelta clays which underlie the distributaries, is approximately 300 ft (91 m). The average rate of discharge of the present-day Mississippi River is about 600,000 cu ft/second (16,800 m³/second). During short periods of intensive storm conditions, rates of discharge as great as 1,350,000 cu ft/second (37,800 m³/second) have been noted (Cobb, 1952). Fisk *et al.* (1954) determined that the suspended load of the river consists of approximately "7 per cent sand, 38 per cent silt, and 55 per cent clay." Scruton (1960) stated that, "The load consists of about 50 per cent clay, 48 per cent silt, and only about 2 per cent sand." Although Fisk's and Scruton's figures for grain-size percentages are at variance, the very low sand content in both estimates is noteworthy. It is equally significant that a little more than 99 percent of the sand fraction is fine grained to very fine grained in texture. The average annual suspended load that the Mississippi River transports to the Gulf of Mexico was estimated by Holle (1952) to be 400 million tons. To this figure he added 25 percent as an estimate of the bed load, bringing the total estimate to 500 million tons per year. Upon reaching the Gulf the sediment is fractionated during deposition. Maximum rates of deposition are 1–1.5 ft/year (0.3–0.5 m/year) near shore and 0.1 ft/year (0.03 m/year) seaward.

Topset Beds

According to Scruton (1960), the topset beds

. . . consist of marsh deposits and delta-front silts and sands, together with related channel, natural levee, and crevasse deposits, and clays and shell beds of the inter-distributary bays, lakes and tidal streams. . . . Lateral and vertical relations are both gradational and sharp. Deep scour, torrential deposition, and slow marsh development all are represented in the top-set beds. The presence of sharp sedimentary breaks and general heterogeneity in these beds is in marked contrast to the progressive changes that occur in the other sediment units. . . . Thickness of top-set beds generally are [sic] less than 10 feet near the present shoreline. Channel fills may be more than 150 feet thick, however.

The marsh deposits, consisting of organic-rich clayey silts and silty clay, are located in the interdistributary areas. In the modern Mississippi River delta they are 1–3 ft (0.3–0.9 m) thick.

The delta-front silts and sands are the most widespread component of the delta; they form an almost continuous sheet along the delta front. They result from the combined effects of wave action and longshore currents, which redistribute the sand and silt brought to the shore by the distributary streams. The delta-front sediments are distributed over an area of several hundred square miles as a result of the gradual progradation of the delta.

Some of the smaller distributaries have been abandoned and filled with massive, fine-grained to very fine-grained sand in the lower part. This grades upward into bedded sands, sandy silts, and silty clays.

The natural levees of the subaerial topset beds form ridges on either side of the distributaries. Fisk *et al.* (1954) wrote: "Natural levee deposits form one of the more distinctive groups of sediments in the deltaic plain. They consist of well-bedded, unfossiliferous, clayey silts and silty clays laid down during seasonal floods." Their average height is 10 ft (3.0 m) above sea level. Kolb and Van Lopik (1966) noted that, "Natural levee elevations along the central portions of Bayou La Loutre approximate 12 and 8 feet, respectively." They further noted that "The height, thickness, width, and grain size of the constituent material of the natural levee flanking the present and the abandoned courses of the Mississippi decrease in a down stream direction."

Crevasse deposits are present along the marsh front; they consist of cross-stratified layers of interbedded fine sands and clayey silts. Fisk *et al.* (1954) noted that, "Extensive marshland tracts have developed in some of the troughs as a result of crevassing of distributaries during flood." Coalescing subaqueous subdeltas of silty sand and sandy silt are deposited by distributary streams which radiate from a crevasse outlet. This sediment is entrapped readily where it invades a marshland, which has abundant vegetal material. In addition to the crevasse deposits, other types of sediments are deposited in the interdistributary trough areas. The deeper parts of the troughs contain massive, poorly sorted, silty clays, whereas the peripheral parts of the trough areas consist of layered sandy silts and clayey silts.

Foreset Beds

Scruton (1960) wrote that,

Fore-set beds are the pro-delta silty clays and the relatively coarse sands, silts, and clays formed off the major distributaries. The foreset beds thicken from a feather edge on the north to a maximum of approximately 250 feet near Southwest Pass; seaward thickening that develops as the delta builds outward into deeper water occurs mostly in the pro-delta silty clay unit.

Fisk *et al.* (1954) stated that, "Sediments of these facies form a belt of fine-grained deposits covering the delta front and the surrounding Gulf floor. They are arbitrarily divided into an inner and outer zone by the line between silty clays and clays shown on the map [Fig. 93]; in the bulge areas they grade into bar 'sands.'" The sediments of the inner zone are transitional with bar "sands." The seaward progradation of the foreset beds is diagrammatically shown in

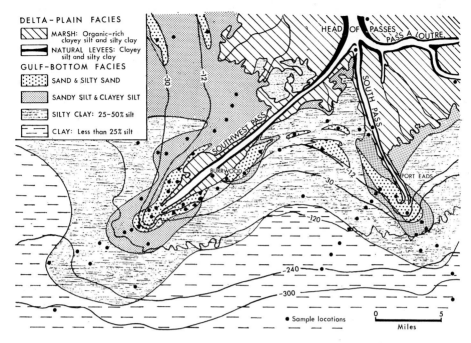

DELTA-PLAIN FACIES

MARSH: Organic-rich clayey silt and silty clay

NATURAL LEVEES: Clayey silt and silty clay

GULF-BOTTOM FACIES

SAND & SILTY SAND

SANDY SILT & CLAYEY SILT

SILTY CLAY: 25–50% silt

CLAY: Less than 25% silt

FIG. 93—Generalized distribution of facies within southwestern part of birdfoot-delta platform. Modified from Fisk *et al.* (1954).

Figure 94. The depositional surface of the foreset beds is subparallel with the time lines. The tilt of the foreset beds of Figure 94 is greatly exaggerated. The depositional surface of the foreset beds directly southwest of Southwest Pass slopes about a third of 1° (30 ft/mi). The basinward slope of this surface in the interdistributary trough area between Southwest Pass and South Pass is about a fifth of 1° (18 ft/mi). Thus these slopes are in sharp contrast to the 30° slope of the foresets in the Gilbert-type delta.

Each of the distributaries of the birdfoot delta is underlain by a deep-water bar finger as shown in Figure 95. The bar fingers consist of well-sorted, fine-grained, thinly bedded sand. They grade laterally into silts and clays. There also is a transitional zone at the base, which is thinnest directly below the middle of a bar finger (Fig. 95). These sand bodies are a little longer than the distributaries and are symmetrically biconvex in cross section. They are approximately 4–5 mi (6.4–8.0 km) wide and 200–250 ft (61–76 m) in maximum thickness. Bar fingers are genetically related to lunate bars, which are formed a short distance beyond the distal ends of the several distributaries. The sands of a lunate bar normally are deposited, free from silt and clay, to an approximate depth (and thickness) of 50 ft (15 m). After this thickness has been deposited, additional increments of sand cause compression and displacement of the underlying prodelta silts and clays. This process of differential compaction and displacement continues until the axial thickness of the sand is approximately 250

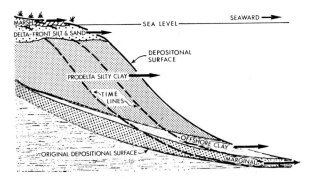

F<small>IG</small>. 94—Seaward migration of depositional environments. With delta growth, different depositional environments migrate seaward and extend the relatively homogeneous sediment units. After Scruton (1960).

ft (76 m). The lunate bar progrades seaward to form a bar finger, as shown in Figure 95. Fisk (1955) wrote:

> As a result, the prograding bar fingers have a biconvex outline in cross section. After the distributary mouth has been extended still farther seaward, the bar deposits continue to settle while natural levees above them are being constructed by overflow waters. The natural levees flanking the distributary channel, incised along the axis of each bar finger, are thickest at the channel margin; consequently the main mass of the levee lies directly over the thick part of the bar finger, and the combined weight of the bar finger sands and the levee deposits contributes to the compaction of the underlying pro-delta sediments. With long-continued subsidence, the upper surface of the bar eventually becomes deeply buried beneath fresh- and brackish-water deposits.

It should be noted that these 250-ft-thick, 4–5-mi-wide (76 m, 6.4–8.0 km) bar-finger sands are not deposited in abandoned distributary channels. Rather, they are extensive, biconvex lenses of well-sorted sand which are much wider than the distributaries which they underlie. For this reason, they are not considered to be channel sands.

Bottomset Beds

The maximum thickness of the bottomset beds is probably 20–30 ft (6.1–9.1 m). Although they are formed partly from river-borne sediments, margin deposits probably should not be combined with offshore clays in defining the bottomset beds, because they are not found in deeper water south of the delta.

Mudlumps

Mudlumps are small, irregularly shaped, ephemeral islands of silty clay and clay which "boil up" near the mouths of the distributaries. They also are known to intrude the unconsolidated sands of bar fingers. They commonly are intricately folded and faulted and may rise as much as 10 ft (3.0 m) above sea level. Morgan (1951) considered them to be vertically displaced clays and silty clays of the foreset beds which rise in response to the vertical settling of the distal

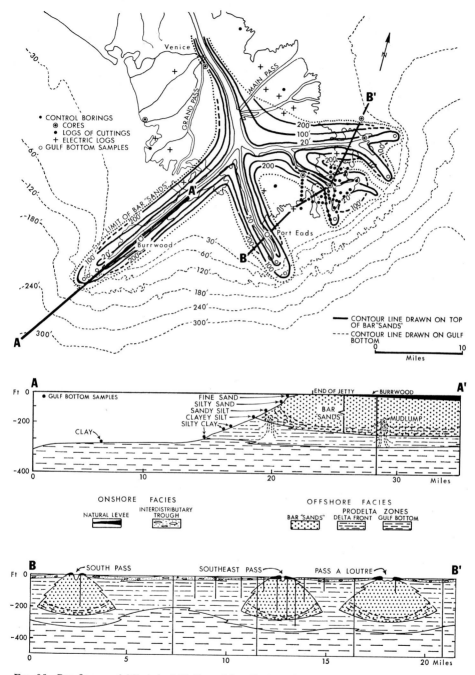

FIG. 95—Bar fingers of Mississippi birdfoot delta. Cross-section *A-A'* is a longitudinal section of Southwest Pass bar finger; cross-section *B-B'* shows bar fingers underlying South Pass, Southeast Pass, and Pass à Loutre. After Fisk *et al.* (1954).

ends of the bar-finger sands. Marine faunas known to have lived at 300–400-ft (91–122 m) water depths have been found in the clays of these mudlumps.

Mississippi River Deltaic Plain

The deltaic plain of the Mississippi River consists of a composite of six or seven deltaic complexes, all of which have been deposited during the past 5,000 years. The sequential positions of delta deposition are numbered on Figure 96, which is modified after Gould and Morgan (1962). The dates of initial occupancy of these positions are shown in the upper right-hand corner of this figure. Each of these deltas is the result of a significant shift in the course of the Mississippi River.

The birdfoot (Balize) delta is strikingly different from the other deltas which preceded it. The premodern deltas are roughly arcuate in outline, are larger, and have many more distributaries than the birdfoot delta. Internal differences are equally striking and appear to have a real bearing on exploration for birdfoot and arcuate deltas in the subsurface. Kolb and Van Lopik (1966) observed that,

In the earlier deltaic deposits sands are restricted to thin, fairly widespread, distributary front layers and to thick, narrow fillings of distributary channels. Sands

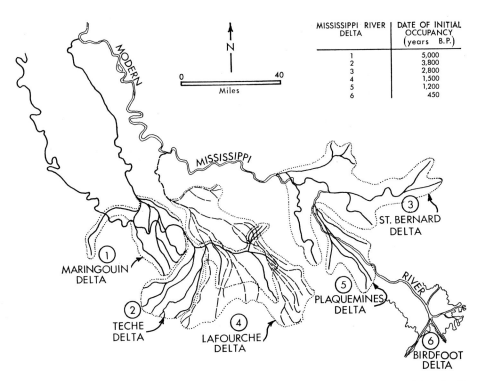

MISSISSIPPI RIVER DELTA	DATE OF INITIAL OCCUPANCY (years B.P.)
1	5,000
2	3,800
3	2,800
4	1,500
5	1,200
6	450

Fig. 96—Sequence of river-course and delta development of Mississippi deltaic plain. After Gould and Morgan (1962).

in the modern (birdfoot) delta are found in wide, thick fingers* which underlie the major distributaries. These dissimilarities between ancient and modern deltas are thought to result from differences in depth of water into which each prograded. The modern Balize Delta has developed near the edge of the continental shelf in water originally reaching depths greater than 300 feet. In contrast, borings in the Lafourche and St. Bernard deltaic complexes indicate that progradation occurred in water ranging in depth from 30 to 150 feet.

The widespread distributary-front layers of sand mentioned in the above quotation are called "delta-front sheet sands" by Fisk (1955). A 300-sq mi (777 km²) delta-front sheet sand, ranging from 20 to 80 ft (6.0–24.4 m) in thickness, underlies the eastern subdelta of the Lafourche delta (Fig. 97). Such sands are picked up at the distal ends of the distributaries by wave action and longshore currents and are redistributed along the entire delta front. Then, as the deltaic mass progrades, the delta-front sand spreads as a regressive sheet. Shoal, or shallow-water, conditions are ideal for the deposition of such a sand body. The source sands for delta-front sheet sands must come from depths no greater than wave base, which is approximately 30 ft (9.1 m) under normal conditions. Where these sheet sands have thicknesses which exceed the depth of wave base, they have compacted and displaced underlying prodelta clays.

The pre-Balize deltas of the Mississippi River deltaic plain all are thought to have been deposited in shoal environments, a factor that favored the development of numerous distributaries. Fisk (1955) wrote:

> These old streams scoured deep narrow channels like that of the present Mississippi River upstream where its beds and banks are composed of silts and clays. Such channels are in marked contrast to the relatively wide and shallow distributary channels of the birdfoot delta which was scoured in bar finger sands [Fig. 95]. As the pre-modern delta fronts advanced, distributaries bifurcated as they lengthened, giving rise to complicated channel patterns and dividing interdistributary troughs into a large number of small basins. . . . Distributaries were abandoned rapidly during delta growth and became plugged with well-sorted sand channel fillings which make up narrow, thick sand bodies characteristic of the shoal-water delta complexes.

When a distributary is abandoned, according to Kolb and Van Lopik (1966),

> Wedges of sand are built at the point where the distributary leaves the main course. These extend for variable distances downstream. In the large abandoned Metairie distributary of the Mississippi that extends through New Orleans, the few borings available indicate a sand wedge filling the bottom of the abandoned distributary that extends downstream for a distance of about 9 miles (Kolb and Van Lopik, 1958a). Overlying this sand wedge is a complementary wedge of fine grained material. It is doubtful if a sand wedge of such size is developed in any but the largest distributaries. However, deep, narrow, sand-filled distributaries are known to exist in the abandoned Lafourche Delta. . . . Present indications are that materials form-

---

* According to J. R. Van Lopik (written commun., February 6, 1974), "a better description would be 'wide, thick pods forming discontinuous fingers.'"

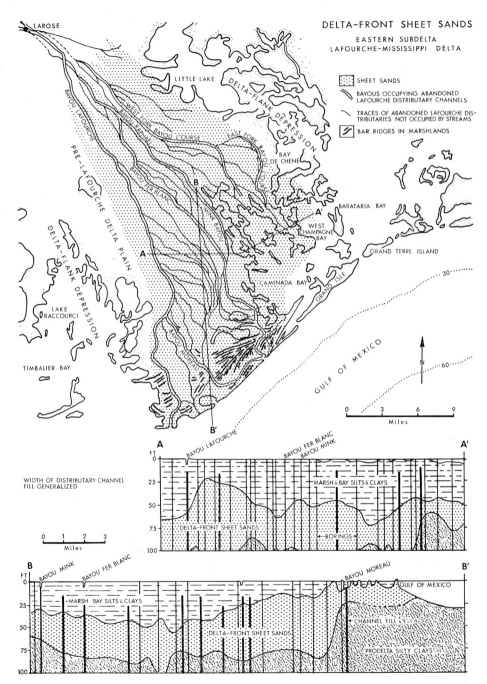

FIG. 97—Delta-front sheet sands in eastern subdelta of Lafourche-Mississippi delta. After Fisk (1955).

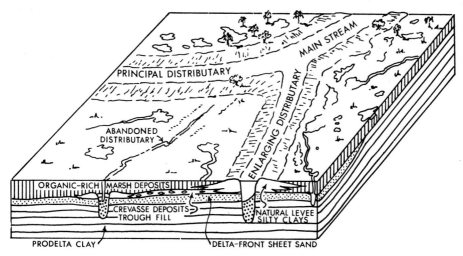

FIG. 98—Depositional sequence in a shoal delta, showing how channels are incised through delta-front sheet sands and even into underlying prodelta clay. Modified after Fisk (1960).

ing the distributary fill are highly variable but a wedge of relatively coarse material, compared to the remainder of the distributary fill, always plugs the upstream end.

Most of the distributaries erode down through the delta-front sheet sands and even into the underlying prodelta clays, as illustrated in Figure 98. When these channels become clogged with sand, silt, and clay, the net effect is one of a sheet sand locally interrupted by linear trends of locally thick sand, thickened primarily at the expense of the underlying clay. Some of the known ancient delta sandstones clearly exhibit this characteristic. The Lafourche delta (Fig. 97) had a great number of major distributaries which Kolb and Van Lopik say ". . . were so closely spaced that intradeltaic deposits form a fairly continuous sandy sequence without intervening clays."

Delta-Margin Island Sands

With each of the at least half dozen times the Mississippi River has shifted its course, a new site of delta formation was established. When a delta site is abandoned, compaction of the underlying prodelta foreset muds continues and subsidence of the delta surface ensues. Wave and longshore-current activity continues to redistribute the sediments of the abandoned delta margin. Scruton (1960) pointed out that, "The most obvious change in the old delta is the presence of a large body of water where there once was marshland." When the river is no longer contributing sediment to the delta margin, waves and longshore currents rework the unconsolidated sediments, removing the silt and clay, and build up an arcuate barrier island. This island is convex seaward and separates the inundated portion of the old delta from the open sea. The barrier island continues to grow as the delta sediments subside by compaction. Scruton (1960) said, "The sorting and concentration process is most active in shallow water where waves are most effective and where most of the sand originally

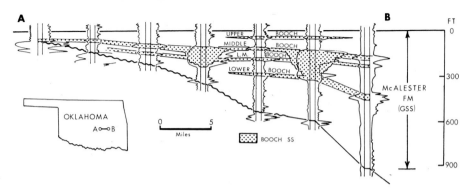

F<small>IG</small>. 99—Correlation of Booch sandstone members of McAlester Formation (Pennsylvanian), western part of Arkoma basin.

was deposited, but it extends down into 30–50 feet of water off the Chandeleurs." The Chandeleurs form an island arc off the St. Bernard–Plaquemines delta complex and separate the Chandeleur and Breton Sounds from the open sea. Other barrier islands are near the original margins of other deltas of the ancestral Mississippi. Their genetic relation to delta margins is considered to be significant in the search for their subsurface counterparts that are related to ancient deltas.

A<small>NCIENT</small> D<small>ELTAS</small>

Only a limited number of ancient deltas have been clearly recognized and described in geologic literature, even though considerable amounts of oil and gas have been produced from sandstones directly related to such deposits. Their extreme range in size, shape, and facies types may explain why they have not been recognized more frequently. This discussion is based on several such deltas which the writer has studied. Some ancient deltas are quite large and produce oil and gas only from very limited parts, whereas others are small in geographic extent and produce hydrocarbons almost everywhere distributary sandstones are present.

Booch Delta[*]

In Early Pennsylvanian time a large delta was deposited in the eastern Oklahoma portion of the Arkoma basin. The main bulk of this delta covers an area of approximately 2,000 sq mi (5,180 km²). It was deposited largely under shoal conditions in a shelf environment. In analyzing the sandstones making up this delta, it is necessary first to consider the genetic sequence of strata of which they are component parts. To do this, a series of stratigraphic profiles, such as that illustrated in Figure 99, was constructed across each of the tiers of townships shown in Figure 101. These profiles then were tied together by an intersecting series of north-south stratigraphic profiles. All wells not used in the

---

[*] This section and the two following sections are taken essentially from an earlier paper by the writer (Busch, 1971, p. 1139–1149).

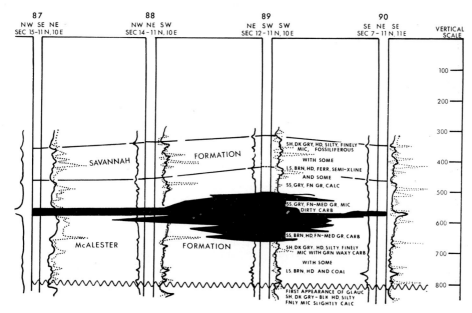

Fig. 100—Correlation of Booch sandstone (black), showing downward thickening of a channel sandstone. Note slight thinning of shale interval directly above thickest part of channel sandstone.

construction of the correlation grid then were correlated with the nearest wells of the grid. Thus the upper and lower limits of the McAlester Formation (genetic sequence of strata) were determined as a prelude to constructing an isopach map of this formation.

Figure 99 is an electric-log cross section of the McAlester Formation in the greater Seminole district of Oklahoma; the cross section illustrates the rate of thickening of this unit as it spread across the northwest shelf area of the Arkoma basin. This wedge of strata is predominantly shale, interrupted by four members of the Booch sandstone. Each of these sandstones is lenticular except the middle Booch member, which appears in Figure 99 to be more sheetlike. This stratigraphic profile is completely misleading, owing to the wide spacing of the control wells. The middle Booch sandstone, for example, is known to increase abruptly in thickness to as much as 250 ft (76 m). In so doing it merges vertically with the lower middle member of the Booch and even with the lower Booch member. The principal direction of thickening is downward, at the expense of the shale which normally separates the middle Booch from the lower middle and lower Booch, respectively. The manner of local thickening of the middle Booch is illustrated in Figure 100, which was constructed in an area where neither the lower middle nor lower Booch was deposited. The maximum thickness of the middle Booch sandstone is 150 ft (46 m), and about 90 percent of the thickening is at the expense of the underlying shale. A slight thinning of the shale interval above the thick sandstone is apparent.

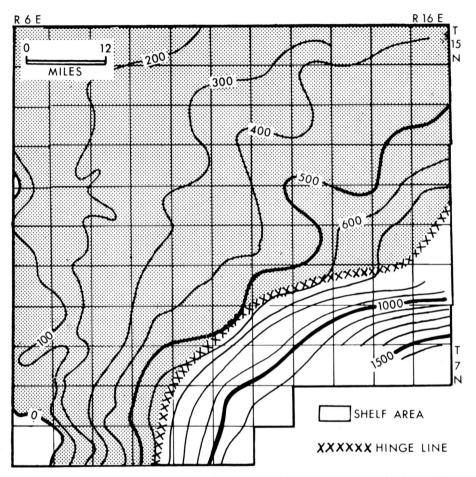

FIG. 101—Isopach map of McAlester Formation, greater Seminole district, eastern Oklahoma. Hinge line separates shelf environment on northwest from more abruptly subsiding basin area on southeast.

The McAlester is overlain conformably by the Savannah Formation, and the shales of these two formations are petrographically indistinguishable. The contact has been placed arbitrarily at an easily recognized reentrant "angle" of the short-normal resistivity curve of the electric logs. This "angle" is present on more than 90 percent of the 650 electric logs available for this study; it occurs about 30 ft (9.1 m) below the base of the unit known as the "Brown lime." This reentrant "angle" is the reference datum of the stratigraphic profile shown in Figures 99 and 100. The base of the McAlester Formation is conformable with the Atoka shale in the more basinward part of the Arkoma basin, but unconformable in the marginal-shelf part of this basin. The McAlester lies unconformably on successively older units to the west, in the direction of the Hunton arch. For example, from southeast to northwest it lies on the Atoka shales and sandstones, on successively older formations of the Morrowan Series,

and on Mississippian shales and limestones along the western margin of the
basin where "post-Atoka" uplift and erosion were the greatest.

Electric-log and sample studies of the McAlester show that the basinward
part (southeast) of this formation consists almost entirely of shale, but in the
area where it is less than 600 ft (183 m) thick it is characterized by an
alternating series of beds of shale, sandstone, limestone, and coal. That the
shelf was never covered by deep water clearly is attested by the presence of
coal beds.

The isopach map of the McAlester Formation (Fig. 101) was drawn for the
purposes of (1) reconstructing the shape of the northwestern part of the Arkoma
depositional basin, (2) determining the trend and position of the "line of
flexure" (hinge line) that existed during McAlester deposition, and (3) ascertain-
ing the principal direction of transport of McAlester sands and mud.

The McAlester Formation thickens abruptly southeast of the "line of flexure"
(Fig. 101) in the part of the basin where subsidence is more pronounced. In
the shelf environment, northwest of the "line of flexure," the southeastward
thickening is much more gradual. The greatest accumulation of sediments
within the mapped area is 1,638 ft (499 m), in T7N, R17E. The trend of the
thickness contour lines changes progressively from northeast-southwest to slightly
west of north. This thickness trend indicates that the northeastern and north-
central parts of the mapped area were progressively more downwarped than the
area to the west during deposition of the McAlester Formation.

Figure 102 is a composite isopach map of the Booch sandstone members of
the McAlester Formation. In the northeastern part of the area (T13–15N,
R14–16E), the upper Booch sandstone is the principal member present. Shaded
areas in the north-central part of the mapped area represent vertical merging
of all four Booch sandstone members. In the region west of R12E, where the
Booch is less than 60 ft (18.3 m) thick, the middle Booch is the principal
sandstone present; all other members are shaly to calcareous siltstones or poorly
developed sandstones. The latter can be correlated only as "horizons" rather
than as lithologic units. The lower middle and lower Booch sandstones are not
present except where merged vertically with other members in the channel areas.

The most pronounced development of sandstone in Figure 102 is in a thick
channel, 3–5 mi (4.8–8.0 km) wide, which trends southeast from T15N,
R11E, to T11N, R14E. The mapped length of this channel sandstone is over
35 mi (56 km) and the maximum thickness exceeds 240 ft (73 m). The sandstone undoubtedly extends much farther southeast, but the data for mapping
it were not available. The thickest parts of this channel sandstone constitute
more than 50 percent of the total thickness of the McAlester Formation; the
rest of the section is predominantly shale. The shale of the McAlester Formation
has been compacted sufficiently, owing to the weight of the overburden, that
the location and trend of this major sandstone can be determined readily from
the isopach map of the McAlester Formation (Fig. 101). As sandstone is
relatively noncompactible, the northwest convexity of the 300-, 400-, and
500-ft contours is due solely to the presence of this prominent distributary-

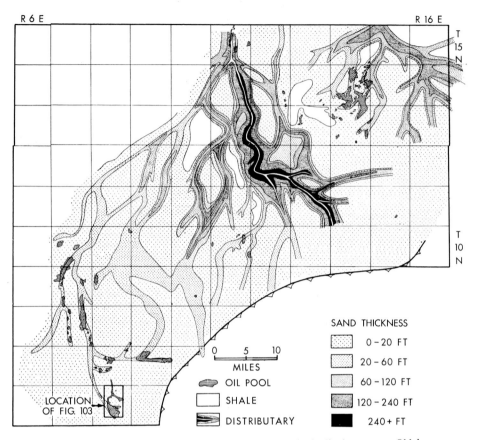

FIG. 102—Isopach map of Booch sandstone, greater Seminole district, eastern Oklahoma.

channel sandstone. This major channel sandstone and the numerous smaller channels of sandstone make up a distributary network of a large delta which had its apex to the north. It is unlikely that all the distributaries shown in Figure 102 were formed simultaneously; this illustration probably represents a composite of all stages of distributary development during McAlester deposition.

The isopach map of the Booch delta (Fig. 102) is based on several thousand electric and drillers' logs. Such a map serves as little more than a geologic framework for more detailed studies. Figure 103, for example, is a more detailed analysis of the Booch reservoir and production in T6N, R8E, for the Hawkins pool. Production is from the middle Booch member, which is directly overlain by a coal bed that shows a characteristic "kick" on the long-normal resistivity curve of the electric logs. The structure contours of Figure 103A describe a sinuous, arcuate high over the pool proper and a narrow, bifurcating structural ridge to the north. The maximum relief over the pool (south half) is approximately 75 ft (22.8 m). In the northern part of the pool the relief

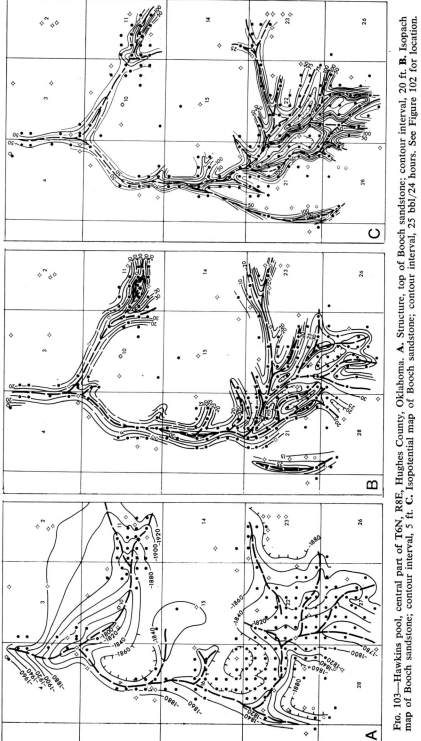

FIG. 103—Hawkins pool, central part of T6N, R8E, Hughes County, Oklahoma. A. Structure, top of Booch sandstone; contour interval, 20 ft. B. Isopach map of Booch sandstone; contour interval, 5 ft. C. Isopotential map of Booch sandstone; contour interval, 25 bbl/24 hours. See Figure 102 for location.

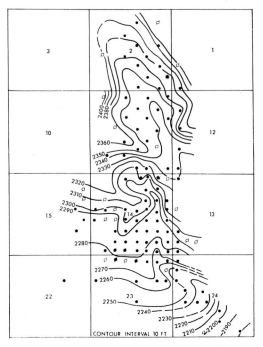

Fig. 104—Structure, Booch sandstone, Wewoka Lake pool, T8N, R7E, greater Seminole district, Oklahoma.

exceeds 120 ft (37 m). Comparison of the trends of structural "highs" (heavy dashed lines) with the axes of maximum sandstone thickness (Fig. 103B) shows that the structure is due partly to variations in sandstone thickness. Logs of wells marginal to the pool show that the Booch is lenslike and that it grades into shale in all directions away from the pool. The base of the coal bed serves as the means of identifying the top of the middle Booch outside the productive area. Figure 103C is an isopotential map of the Booch; the contour interval is 25 bbl. The estimated 24-hour potentials of the wells are more significant when it is realized that the wells were drilled before the advent of hydraulic fracturing. Trends of maximum initial potential (heavy dashed lines) coincide extremely well with trends of maximum sandstone thickness (Fig. 103B). This correlation is to be expected inasmuch as the initial potential is an indirect measure of the relative permeability of the sandstone at any one borehole position. The deltaic aspect of this sandstone is much more apparent from Figure 103B and C than from Figure 103A. Postdepositional tectonism locally has modified the structure of the middle Booch (Fig. 103A); the most pronounced effect is a local structural depression in adjacent parts of Sections 16 and 21. Preparation of such isopach and isopotential maps provides an excellent basis for systematic stepout development drilling. Drill-site locations are selected where axial trends are most likely to extend.

The Wewoka Lake pool is situated in T8N, R7E (Fig. 102). It has a north-south trend within a middle Booch distributary-channel sandstone. Its structural configuration, shown in Figure 104, consists of two irregular, *en échelon* noses which plunge slightly west of north. These noses constitute local interruptions of a regional western dip. There is no evidence of structural closure. Limited thin-section studies of middle Booch samples taken from wells along the eastern margin of this pool have shown that the sandstone is very fine grained and that the interstices are filled with clay. An oil-water contact has not been determined, so it is surmised that all margins of this pool are related to an abrupt decrease in permeability.

There are significant petrographic differences between the distributary-channel sandstones and the interdistributary sheet sandstones, especially in the south-eastern half of the delta (Fig. 102). Where channel sandstones exceed 20 ft (6.1 m) in thickness, they generally have larger mean grain diameters than those of the interchannel areas; the average diameters for the two sandstone types are 99 and 86μ, respectively. The channel sandstones also are better sorted than the interchannel sandstones. In addition to these differences, the sandstones of the interchannel areas have an average clay content of 20 percent, as compared to 15 percent in the channels. The higher percentage of clay and smaller grain size of the sand in the interchannel areas might explain the relative absence of oil in these areas.

The Booch sandstones are very fine grained and are of the graywacke type; that is, they contain abundant fragments of preexisting rocks and relatively abundant clay matrix. The grain-size distribution and standard deviation are illustrated in Figure 105. Petrographic data for the Booch are summarized in Table 4.

Most oil pools in the Booch sandstone are not in the thick channel sandstones but, rather, in the thinner channel sandstones. An irregular cluster of oil pools

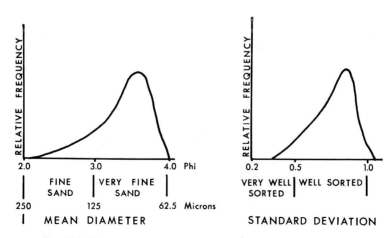

FIG. 105—Mean diameter and standard deviation of Booch sandstone.

Table 4. Summary of Petrographic Data for Booch Sandstones.

	Range	Average (μ)	No. Samples
Mean Grain Diam. (μ)	71–91	83	28
Stand. Deviation (ϕ)	0.34–1.01	0.76	28
% Clastic quartz	45–90	54	36
% Carbonate	0–33	4	36
% Clay	2–40	16	36
% Rock fragments	9–50	22	36
% Secondary silica	9–50	22	36
% Other minerals	0–3	2	36

is located in T13–14N, R14E (Fig. 102), about midway between two main distributary systems. If sufficient log data were available in this area, it probably could be shown that these pools are mostly in thinner distributary-channel sandstones close to shales of a backswamp environment. Several elongate pools are located in distributary-channel sandstones in the southwestern part of Figure 102. None of these pools bear much relation to structure; they probably owe their existence to permeability seals surrounding more porous and permeable parts of channel sandstones. Several significant oil pools (not shown) are located in certain parts of the thicker channel sandstones in the middle part of Figure 102. In this area the channel sandstones are medium to coarse grained and contain less interstitial clay. Such pools occur where the axes of west-plunging structural noses intersect the axes of major distributary-channel sandstones. In this situation, oil-water contacts are readily determined on the north and south sides of the pools, and permeability decreases abruptly on the east and west margins, where the channel sandstones merge with the silty, fine-grained sheet sandstones.

Tonkawa Delta

The uppermost member of the Tonkawa sandstone (upper Missouri Series of the Pennsylvanian) is an excellent example of a gas-bearing deltaic reservoir. The ancient Tonkawa delta is present in Beaver County in the Oklahoma Panhandle part of the Anadarko basin. This delta was described and illustrated in a recent paper by Khaiwka (1968), in which he pointed out that the upper member of the Tonkawa sandstone is overlain by the thin (3 ft or 0.9 m), persistent "Haskell" limestone. Jordan (1957) noted that this thin stratigraphic unit is a marker bed; it is a convenient datum of reference in a stratigraphic analysis of the directly underlying upper member of the Tonkawa. Figure 106A is an electric-log and microlog illustration of the three sandstone members of the Tonkawa and their relation to the "Haskell" limestone. The downward thickening of the upper member of the Tonkawa sandstone relative to the "Haskell" limestone reference datum is illustrated in Figure 106B. This single stratigraphic profile is typical of many that have been drawn in the area, and it illustrates the channel aspect of this sandstone body. Two isopach maps illustrate the distributary-channel network of the upper member of the Tonkawa sandstone. Khaiwka (1968) illustrated the distribution pattern of this sandstone by constructing an isopach map of the stratigraphic interval between the "Haskell" limestone and the base of the upper sandstone member; this interval is actually a genetic increment of strata (Fig. 107). He pointed out that, "This map is essentially a submarine, paleotopographic map showing a deltaic distributary system of channels . . . it is thickest where down-cutting was at a maximum; the respective valley axes are drawn along these trends of maximum down-cutting (greatest thickness)." The maximum well density is one well per section; therefore, only a generalized interpretation is possible.

Using Figure 107 as a guide, Khaiwka made a subjective interpretation of the thickness variations of the upper member of the Tonkawa sandstone (Fig. 108). In discussing this latter map, Khaiwka pointed out that, "Locally deltaic distributaries migrated laterally, such as in the 'four-corner area' of T's 3 and 4 N., R's 24 and 25 ECM; southwestern corner of T. 4 N., R. 26 ECM; T. 3 N., R. 27 ECM; and T. 2 N., R's 24 and 25 ECM." Thus, the trends of maximum sandstone thickness do not coincide everywhere with trends of maximum downcutting. The thickness of the upper sandstone member of the Tonkawa ranges from 0 to 35 ft (0–10.7 m). The upper surface is relatively flat and the basal surface is quite irregular. Interdistributary areas commonly are blanketed with thinner sandstone, all of which has reservoir capabilities.

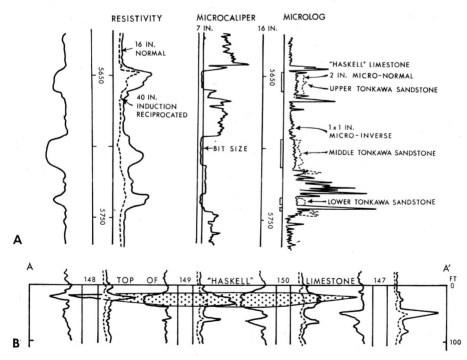

FIG. 106—**A.** Electric log and micrologs, showing three members of Tonkawa sandstone and their stratigraphic positions relative to "Haskell" limestone. **B.** Stratigraphic cross-section *A-A'* of upper Tonkawa sandstone, showing downward thickening at expense of underlying shale. Reference datum is top of "Haskell" limestone. See Figure 107 for location of cross section.

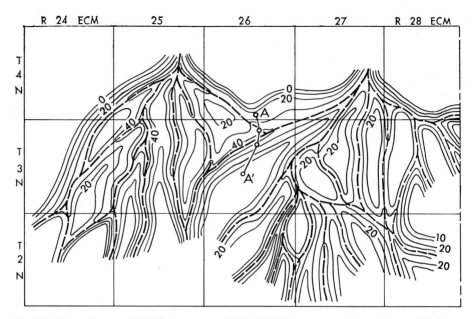

Fig. 107—Isopach map of GIS between top of "Haskell" limestone and base of upper Tonkawa sandstone, Beaver County, Oklahoma. This map shows two laterally coalescing distributary systems. Contour interval, 10 ft. After Khaiwka (1968).

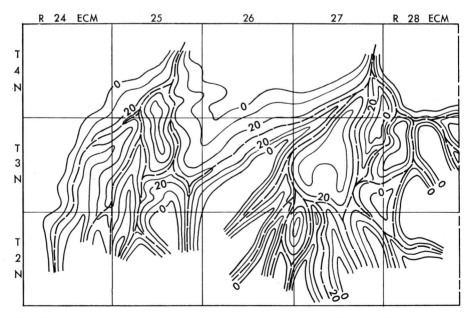

Fig. 108—Isopach map of upper Tonkawa sandstone, Beaver County, Oklahoma. Contour interval, 10 ft. After Khaiwka (1968).

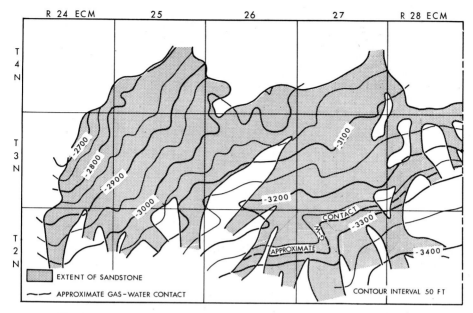

FIG. 109—Structure map, top of Tonkawa sandstone, Beaver County, Oklahoma.

The gas distribution in the upper member of the Tonkawa sandstone is controlled by a combination of sandstone distribution and structure, as illustrated in Figure 109. Gas migrated north-northwest until it reached the updip extent of the sandstone. A gas-water contact can be noted at the approximate position of −3,270 ft (−997 m).

This type of regional stratigraphic analysis would have been of considerable benefit to the explorationist during the development of this pool. Preferential locations where sandstone was thickest above the gas-water contact could have been predicted readily once the depositional nature of the sandstone had been ascertained.

Endicott Delta

The Endicott sandstone, in the lower Virgil Series of the Pennsylvanian in Harper County, Oklahoma, is an excellent example of a subsurface deltaic sandstone. It was deposited in a series of bifurcating distributary channels which were eroded into the north flank of the Anadarko basin. Regional depositional strike during Virgil deposition was west-northwest and the regional dip was south-southwest.

The Endicott sandstone in this area lies unconformably on either the Toronto limestone or the unnamed shale directly underlying the Toronto, as illustrated in Figure 110. This illustration shows that the principal direction of thickening of the Endicott is downward. Because these profiles are "hung" on the Oread Limestone reference datum, the Lovell sandstone, "Haskell" limestone, and Tonkawa sandstone, respectively, are bowed downward directly under the wells

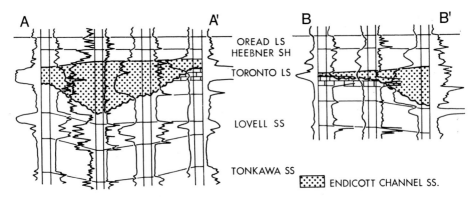

FIG. 110—Stratigraphic profiles showing channel nature of Endicott sandstone, northwestern Oklahoma. Toronto limestone is eroded away at positions of maximum sandstone thickness. See Figure 111 for location of profiles.

exhibiting maximum Endicott channel fill. This distortion is attributed primarily to differential compaction of the shale section separating the Toronto limestone from the Lovell sandstone. That differential compaction of this shale was concurrent with deposition of the Heebner shale (above the Endicott sandstone) is indicated by a tendency for the Heebner to be thinner over areas of thick Endicott and, conversely, to be thicker in areas of thinner Endicott. This thickening and thinning is the result of compensatory deposition in areas of slightly deeper water. A single apparent exception to this principle appears in the easternmost well of profile A-A', Figure 110. It is explained by the fact that a remnant of the Toronto limestone is preserved under the Endicott in this well, and in all probability would not compact any more than the Endicott itself.

The Oread Limestone is an excellent marker bed in this area, and it serves as the upper limit of a genetic increment of strata which extends downward to the unconformity at the base of the Endicott channel fill. An isopach map of this genetic increment of strata (Fig. 111) presents a "cast" of the erosion surface present immediately before deposition of Endicott sandstone. This irregular surface largely controlled the positions of linear trends of thick Endicott sandstone. The axial trends of maximum downcutting before Endicott deposition are indicated by bifurcating dashed lines. The composite picture is that of a deltaic complex consisting of two laterally merging deltas which fan out to the south.

Khaiwka (1968) pointed out that "Caps (1959), and later Winter (1963), depicted the Endicott as a blanket-type sandstone." This characterization is correct if one considers only the generally smooth, rather extensive upper surface of the Endicott. The thickness of this formation varies, however, from 0 to more than 180 ft (55 m), and a thickness change of as much as 100 ft (30 m) in a distance of 1 mi (1.6 km) is not unusual. Khaiwka prepared an isopach map of the Endicott (not published, but inspected by the writer) which is almost identical with Figure 111 insofar as trends of maximum thickness are concerned. He commented (personal commun.) that, "This similarity indicates that there was little or no migration of the deltaic distributaries. The thalwegs of the individual distributaries, with their bifurcating pattern, almost coincide on the two isopach maps." He believes that, "The Endicott delta probably was deposited adjacent to a coastal plain of relatively high relief because sand bodies form major parts of its framework."

On the basis of limited sample and thin-section studies, the Endicott appears to be a gray, poorly sorted, fine-grained, micaceous and calcareous sandstone. Khaiwka has noted 85–90 percent quartz. Locally, the muscovite and chlorite compose as much as 10 percent of the bulk volume. In other areas, as much as 10 percent chert and 5 percent feldspars (mostly plagioclase) have been estimated from thin-section studies. The porosity ranges from fair to good, with a maximum observed value of 18 percent. The sandstone is laminated with light- to dark-gray carbonaceous shales and is overlain by dark-gray and black pyritic shales with coal streaks at the base.

The structure of the Endicott is that of a south-dipping homocline devoid of any significant structural noses or closures. Although the Endicott within the area of Figure 111 has good reservoir characteristics, it apparently lacks the necessary trapping mechanism, such as an updip permeability seal or structural closure. The only known Endicott production occurs from several wells in the Oklahoma and Texas Panhandle parts of the Anadarko basin.

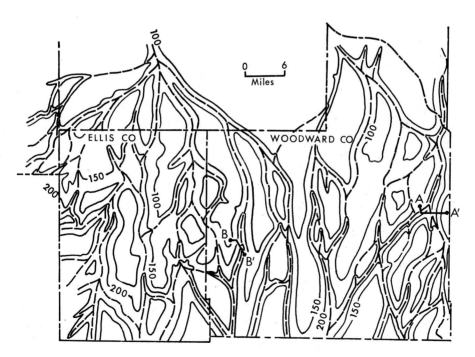

FIG. 111—Isopach map of GIS between top of Oread Limestone and base of Endicott sandstone, northwestern Oklahoma. This is a "cast" of eroded surface upon which Endicott was deposited in area of two laterally coalescing, deltaic distributary systems. Contour interval, 50 ft.

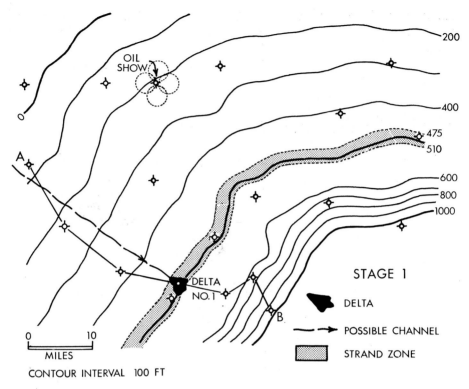

Fig. 112—Stage 1. Hypothetical isopach map of GSS deposited during cyclic subsidence. Oil-bearing sandstone reservoir is shown where ancient drainage course discharged sediment just basinward from stillstand position of shoreline.

DELTA PROSPECTING

Deltas, although varied in size, are seldom isolated phenomena along modern shorelines. Marginal-marine conditions favorable to delta formation at the mouths of rivers generally extend for many miles along the shorelines. Most positive land areas, particularly in humid to semihumid environments, are drained by series of streams flowing to bordering embayments. Although present drainage into the Gulf of Mexico is dominated by the Mississippi and Rio Grande Rivers, there are numerous smaller drainage courses emptying into the Gulf along the Texas-Louisiana coastline.

In order for a delta to form, the shoreline of an embayment must remain relatively stationary. Thus, if a relatively stable shoreline favors development of a delta at the mouth of one river, it also should favor delta development at the mouths of most, if not all, rivers flowing into the same embayment.

If the shoreline is transgressing in response to cyclic subsidence of the basin area (or eustatic rises in sea level), conditions are ideal for the formation of rows of deltas at the successive stillstand positions of the shoreline. Likewise, conditions for delta preservation are ideal when the shoreline transgresses in a cyclic manner. This situation can be illustrated best by reference to a hypothetical diagram (Fig. 112), which shows Stage 1 of a series of three stages portraying a method of prospecting for ancient deltas. Figure 112 is an isopach map of a genetic sequence of strata that includes the oil-productive sandstone of delta No. 1. This GSS was picked after constructing a series of stratigraphic profiles which collectively form a correlation grid of the area. The productive sandstone(s) of delta No. 1 occurs either at, or very near, the GSS base, which is defined by an unconformity. The isopach map of this GSS shows fairly uniform southeastward thickening. Marine transgression was from southeast to northwest, and the depositional strike of the shoreline was northeast.

A detailed stratigraphic analysis of delta No. 1 reveals that the oil-productive sandstones consist of a series of southeastward-diverging channel fills. All of the channel sandstones may be at the same stratigraphic position relative to the marker bed at the top of the GSS, or they may be at several closely spaced intervening levels relative to the marker bed. This system of distributary channels is identified as either a single or a composite ancient deltaic complex. Its apex is approximately at the position of the 475-ft (145 m) isopach (dotted), and its southeastern margin is at about the 510-ft (155 m) isopach. Thus, the reservoir sandstones of delta No. 1 were deposited in a strand zone (shown by stippling). This strand zone is, of necessity, subparallel with the nearest contour lines of the isopach map of the GSS. Because several deltas are likely to have been deposited simultaneously at the mouths of rivers which emptied into the embayment along this strand zone, there may be several prospective reservoirs along the stippled zone. Three dry holes already have been drilled within this zone, so additional information is needed in order to prospect intelligently.

It is a relatively safe assumption that a drainage course extended northwest from the apex of delta No. 1 and that its trend was essentially normal to the depositional strike. Delta No. 1 is located where this projected drainage course intersects the strand zone. If additional drainage courses could be recognized, similar areas of intersection would be highly promising. A review of all existing log and test data reveals stratigraphically higher sandstone development (with an oil show) in a well approximately 30 mi (48 km) north, in the northwest part of Figure 112. Well samples show oil staining and a drill-stem test recovered oil in noncommercial quantity. This well appears to be on the edge of a pool, but which edge is not known. Four possible pool outlines are indicated with dotted circles.

At this early stage of regional analysis, it is necessary to drill a sufficient number of stepout wells from this dry hole to find the pool.

Because delta No. 1 produces from a distributary system deposited during one of the stillstands of a shoreline during cyclic subsidence, the sandstone of delta No. 2 (Fig. 113) probably was deposited under similar conditions at a later stage of cyclic subsidence. In Figure 113 the position, outline, and nature of the reservoir sandstone(s) of delta No. 2 have been determined. The drainage course of this delta is projected northwestward, normal to the paleodepositional strike. Marine transgression has little or no effect on the position of a drainage course; thus it is reasonable to project the drainage through delta No. 2 in a southeast direction. This projected drainage course intersects the strand zone on the southeast within the area labeled "Delta Prospect No. 1."

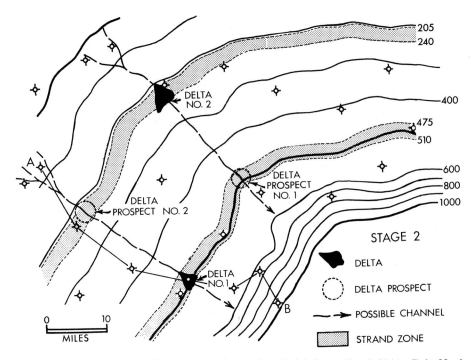

Fig. 113—Stage 2. Hypothetical isopach map of strata deposited during cyclic subsidence. Delta No. 1 and delta prospect No. 1 are located where drainage channels intersect a strand zone, and delta No. 2 and delta prospect No. 2 are located where headward projections of drainage channels are crossed by another strand zone.

At this stage of regional analysis, delta prospect No. 2 assumes the same significance as delta prospect No. 1. It, too, lies within the area of intersection of a projected drainage course and an established strand zone.

It is reasonable to assume that, by the time delta prospects Nos. 1 and 2 have been discovered and developed, numerous additional dry holes (and possibly discovery wells) will have been drilled within the area. The new data afford the means of much more detailed stratigraphic analysis and prospecting. With additional data, many more pools (of various types) may be anticipated. For example, if the unconformity surface at the base of the GSS is fairly smooth, additional drainage channels (with deltas) should be anticipated on the east and southwest, with spacing similar to that between the two postulated channels. Additional strand zones southeast of the first strand zone, and possibly between the two established strand zones, should be anticipated.

A generalized stratigraphic profile of the GSS between delta No. 1 and delta prospect No. 2 (profile *A-B*, Fig. 114) will serve as a basis for determining the thickness of the shale interval between the "pay" sandstones of the two established strand zones. If this shale interval is 50 ft (15.2 m) thick or more, it is reasonable to postulate at least one more strand zone between the sandstones. Nonproductive sandstones in the dry holes between these two strand zones are indications of other strand zones.

Additional well data will permit determination of the smoothness of the unconformity surface, as well as its basinward tilt at the time of the cyclic marine transgression. In Figure 113 the strand zones are approximately 20 mi (32 km) apart, and the amount of GSS thickening is 270 ft (82 m). A 13.5-ft/mi (2.6 m/km) thickening strongly suggests the presence of several more strand zones between the two established zones. A cyclic change in sea level (or subsidence) totaling 25–50 ft (7.6–15.2 m) is much more likely than a 270-ft (82 m) change.

With the acquisition of additional drilling data, it is possible to define clearly the strand positions present within the study area. This is accomplished by reducing the contour interval of the GSS to 50 ft (15.2 m), or possibly 20 ft (6.1 m). Because this GSS is, in a sense, a "cast" of the unconformity surface, the contour lines will bend upstream as illustrated in Figure 115. Selective parts of these channels may be clogged with sandstone, thus affording ideal conditions for oil and gas reservoirs of the simple channel type or, possibly, the point-bar type.

Figure 115 shows that additional well control made it possible to delineate more strand zones and, as a result, to locate and develop additional deltaic reservoirs. The newly discovered strand zones on the southeast overlap because of the abrupt increase in the rate of thickening of the GSS on the seaward side of the hinge line. In such areas of steeper gradient there is less lateral shift of the shoreline in response to cyclic subsidence. Consequently, a part of one delta actually might overlap the apical part of an earlier delta. In such areas,

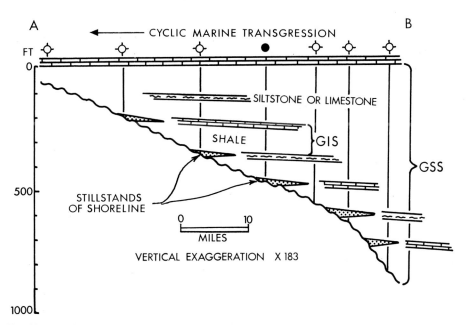

Fig. 114—Stratigraphic profile *A-B* of hypothetical GSS, showing sandstone development at succession of stillstand positions of shoreline. Location is shown on Figure 115.

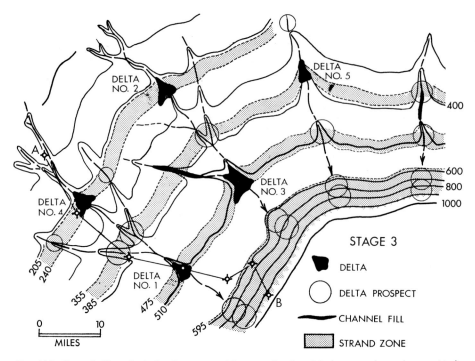

Fig. 115—Stage 3. Hypothetical paleotopographic map, showing deltaic reservoirs and prospects in areas of intersection of strand zones and paleodrainage zones. Individual oil pools in channel sandstone also are shown.

the individual strand zones are likely to be narrower than on the shelf, but the sandstones are likely to be thicker.

Where longshore currents were operative in redistributing sediments furnished at river mouths, beach sands may have been deposited. Such beach sandstones commonly are gas bearing, for reasons not currently understood. Examples are the Clinton (Lower Silurian) sandstones of east-central Ohio, Atoka (Pennsylvanian) sandstones of east-central Oklahoma, Morrowan (Pennsylvanian) sandstones of northwest Oklahoma and northern Texas, and the Mesaverde (Cretaceous) sandstones of northwestern New Mexico.

The interpretation idealized in Figure 115 (Stage 3) presents many additional prospects for exploration drilling. In construction of the figure, all postdepositional structure has been removed. With data theoretically available for the construction of Figure 115, however, it would be a simple matter to make a structural map, preferably with the lithologic-time marker bed at the top of the GSS as datum. Thus, the modifying effect of possible structures on accumulation of hydrocarbons could be determined readily. In this hypothetical example, the prime emphasis is one of predicting areas favorable for reservoir-sandstone development, whether of deltaic distributaries, subaerial channel sandstones, or beach deposits. At this stage the exploration geologist is ready to determine the possible modifying effects of postdepositional structure on oil and gas accumulation.

bibliography

General

American Commission on Stratigraphic Nomenclature, 1948
Barton, D. C., 1930
Bernard, H. A., and R. J. LeBlanc, 1965
Bernard, H. A., R. J. LeBlanc, and C. F. Major, 1962
Bernard, H. A., *et al.*, 1970
Bullard, F. M., 1942
Calvert, W. L., 1962, 1963
Curray, J. R., F. J. Emmel, and P. J. S. Crampton, 1969
Dapples, E. C., W. C. Krumbein, and L. L. Sloss, 1948
Duboul-Razavet, C., 1956
Fisk, H. N., and E. McFarlan, Jr., 1955
Flores, R. M., 1967
Gary, M., R. McAfee, Jr., and C. L. Wolf, eds., 1972
Goldstein, A., Jr., 1942
Greenman, N. N., and R. J. LeBlanc, 1956
Hollenshead, C. T., and R. L. Pritchard, 1961
Howell, J. V., chm., 1960
Johnson, K. G., and G. M. Friedman, 1969
Jordan, L., 1957
Krumbein, W. C., 1945, 1948
Lagaaij, R., and F. P. H. W. Kopstein, 1964
Leatherock, C., 1937
Lohse, E. A., 1955
Lowman, S. W., 1949
Martin, R., 1966
Nanz, R. N., 1954
Peterson, J. A., and J. C. Osmond, eds., 1961
Powers, W. E., 1958

Price, W. A., 1954a
Rainwater, E. H., 1963a
Reineck, H. E., 1967
Shepard, F. P., 1937
Sverdrup, H. U., M. W. Johnson, and R. H. Fleming, 1942
Swann, D. H., 1964
van Straaten, L. M. J. U., 1954
von Engeln, O. D., and K. E. Caster, 1952
Wanless, H. R., 1931
Weirich, T. E., 1953
Weller, J. M., 1930, 1956

Barrier Bars

Bass, N. W., 1934, 1958
Bass, N. W., *et al.*, 1937
Bernard, H. A., C. F. Major, Jr., and B. S. Parrott, 1959
Bernard, H. A., *et al.*, 1970
Blanton, S. L., 1963
Conatser, W. E., 1971
Curray, J. R., 1956
Davis, R. A., Jr., and W. T. Fox, 1972
Dodge, C. F., 1965
Élie de Beaumont, L., 1845
Evans, O. F., 1942
Fisher, J. J., 1968
Fisk, H. N., 1959
Gilbert, G. K., 1885
Gould, H. R., 1972
Griffith, E. G., 1966
Hobday, D. K., and J. G. Reading, 1972
Hoyt, J. H., 1967, 1968, 1970
Hoyt, J. H., and V. J. Henry, Jr., 1965, 1967

Hoyt, J. H., R. J. Weimer, and V. J. Henry, Jr., 1964
Hoyt, J. H., *et al.*, 1952
Johnson, D. W., 1919
Khaiwka, M. H., 1968, 1973
King, C. A. M., 1959
Kuenen, Ph. H., 1950
LeBlanc, R. J., and W. D. Hodgson, 1959a, b, 1961
Leontyev, O. K., and L. G. Nikiforov, 1966
McKee, E. D., and T. S. Sterrett, 1961
Miller, D. N., Jr., 1962
Mothersill, J. S., 1969
Otvos, E. G., Jr., 1970a, b
Pepper, J. F., *et al.*, 1944, 1955
Phleger, F. B, and G. C. Ewing, 1962
Sabins, F. F., Jr., 1963
Schwartz, M. L., 1972
Shepard, F. P., 1950a
Shepard, F. P., and D. G. Moore, 1955a, b
Thompson, W. O., 1937
Todd, T. W., 1968
van Straaten, L. M. J. U., 1965
Zenkovich, V. P., 1962

Beach Sands

Bascom, W. N., 1954
Beall, A. O., Jr., 1968
Bluck, B. J., 1967
Bradley, W. C., 1957
Campbell, C. V., 1971
Cherry, J. A., 1966
Choubert, B., 1948
Cotton, C. A., 1954
Friedman, G. M., 1967
Geyskes, D. C., 1948
Gresswell, R. K., 1957
Guilcher, A., 1958, 1959
Guillou, R. B., and J. J. Glass, 1957
Hedgpeth, J. W., 1947
Kuenen, Ph. H., 1959
LeBlanc, R. J., and W. D. Hodgson, 1959a, b
Lynch, S. A., 1954
McCurdy, P. G., 1947
McGill, J. T., 1959
Nota, D. J. G., 1958
Pincus, H. J., 1959, 1960
Price, W. A., 1951, 1954b
Pugh, J. C., 1953
Shepard, F. P., 1948, 1950b, 1952
Shepard, F. P., and D. G. Moore, 1955a
Sverdrup, H. U., M. W. Johnson, and R. H. Fleming, 1942
Thompson, W. O., 1949
U.S. Congress, 1953
van Straaten, L. M. J. U., 1953, 1957

Channel Sands

Allen, J. R. L., 1965a
Andresen, M. J., 1961, 1962
Ashley, G. H., 1899
Bernard, H. A., and C. F. Major, Jr., 1963
Beutner, E. C., L. A. Gleckinger, and T. M. Gard, 1967
Blench, T., 1951a, b
Boyd, D. R., and B. F. Dyer, 1964
Brune, G. M., 1950

Buckley, A. B., 1922–23
Burnham, W. L., 1956
Busch, D. A., 1959
Coleman, J. M., 1969
Corbett, D. M., *et al.*, 1943
Cross, W. P., and R. H. Bernhagen, 1949
Das, I., 1950
Davis, W. M., 1899, 1902
Einstein, H. A., 1950
Einstein, H. A., and N. L. Barbarossa, 1951
Eisenstatt, P., 1960
Ellison, W. D., 1945
Fisk, H. N., 1944, 1947
Frazier, D. E., and A. Osanik, 1961
Friedman, S. A., 1960
Gilbert, G. K., 1914
Glymph, L. M., 1951
Griffith, W. M., 1927
Griggs, G. B., and L. D. Kulm, 1970
Hembree, C. H., *et al.*, 1952
Hopkins, M. E., 1958
Horton, R. E., 1945
Hoyt, W. V., 1959
Johnson, J. W., 1943
Kennedy, R. G., 1895
Lacey, G., 1930, 1939
Lane, D. W., 1963
Lane, E. W., 1937
Lane, E. W., and W. M. Borland, 1951
Lara, J. M., and C. R. Miller, 1951
Leopold, L. B., and T. Maddock, Jr., 1953
Lindley, E. S., 1919
Linsley, R. K., *et al.*, 1949
Macklin, J. H., 1948
McKee, E. D., 1957
Pepper, J. F., W. R. de Witt, Jr., and D. F. Demarest, 1954
Potter, P. E., 1962a, b
Potter, P. E., and F. J. Pettijohn, 1963
Price, W. A., 1963
Rich, J. L., 1923
Rubey, W. W., 1933, 1952
Schlee, J. S., and R. H. Moench, 1961
Schumm, S. A., 1972
Schumm, S. A., and H. R. Khan, 1972
Serra, E. F., III, 1950, 1951
Shulits, S., 1941
Siever, R., 1951
Steinmetz, R., 1972
Stevens, J. C., 1937
Thomas, A. R., 1946, 1949
Tinler, K. J., 1971
U.S. Army Corps of Engineers, 1935
U.S. Bureau of Reclamation, 1949
Vanoni, V. A., 1941, 1946
Vice, R. B., and E. F. Serra, III, 1950
Wilson, C. W., Jr., 1948

Chenier Sands

Byrne, J. V., D. O. LeRoy, and C. M. Riley, 1959
Dillard, W. R., D. P. Oak, and N. W. Bass, 1941
Doran, E., Jr., 1955
Fisk, H. N., 1948
Gould, H. R., and E. McFarlan, Jr., 1959
Gould, H. R., and J. P. Morgan, 1962
Hammond, E. H., 1954
Howe, H. V., *et al.*, 1935

REFERENCES

Allen, J. R. L., 1965a, A review of the origin and characteristics of recent alluvial sediments: Sedimentology (spec. issue), v. 5, no. 2, p. 191.

―――― 1965b, Late Quaternary Niger delta, and adjacent areas: sedimentary environments and lithofacies: Am. Assoc. Petroleum Geologists Bull., v. 49, no. 5, p. 547–600.

American Commission on Stratigraphic Nomenclature, 1948, Note 3—Rules of geological nomenclature of the Geological Survey of Canada: Am. Assoc. Petroleum Geologists Bull., v. 32, no. 3, p. 366–367.

Amsden, T. W., 1955, Lithofacies map of Lower Silurian deposits in central and eastern United States: Am. Assoc. Petroleum Geologists Bull., v. 39, p. 60–74.

Andresen, M. J., 1961, Geology and petrology of the Trivoli sandstone in the Illinois Basin: Illinois Geol. Survey Circ. 316, 31 p.

―――― 1962, Paleodrainage patterns: their mapping from subsurface data, and their paleogeographic value: Am. Assoc. Petroleum Geologists Bull., v. 46, no. 3, p. 398–405.

Ashley, G. H., 1899, The coal deposits of Indiana: Indiana Dept. Geology and Nat. Resources, Ann. Rept. 23, p. 1–1573.

Bagnold, R. A., 1941, The physics of blown sand and desert dunes: New York, Wm. Morrow and Co.

Barrell, J., 1912, Criteria for the recognition of ancient delta deposits: Geol. Soc. America Bull., v. 23, p. 377–446.

―――― 1914, The Upper Devonian delta of the Appalachian geosyncline: Am. Jour. Sci., v. 37, p. 87–109, 225–253.

Barton, D. C., 1930, Deltaic coastal plain of southeastern Texas: Geol. Soc. America Bull., v. 41, no. 3, p. 359–382.

Bascom, W. N., 1954, Characteristics of natural beaches, Chap. 10 of J. W. Johnson, ed., 4th Coastal Engineering Conf. Proc., October 1953: p. 163–180.

Bass, N. W., 1934, Origin of Bartlesville shoestring sands, Greenwood and Butler Counties, Kansas: Am. Assoc. Petroleum Geologists Bull., v. 18, no. 10, p. 1333–1342.

―――― 1939, Verden sandstone of Oklahoma—an exposed shoestring sand of Permian age: Am. Assoc. Petroleum Geologists Bull., v. 23, no. 4, p. 559–581.

―――― 1958, Some features common to sand bars on modern coasts and in geologic column (abs.): Am. Assoc. Petroleum Geologists Bull., v. 42, no. 1, p. 210–211.

―――― et al., 1937, Origin and distribution of Bartlesville and Burbank sands in parts of Oklahoma and Kansas: Am. Assoc. Petroleum Geologists Bull., v. 21, no. 1, p. 30–66.

Bates, C. C., 1953, Rational theory of delta formation: Am. Assoc. Petroleum Geologists Bull., v. 37, no. 9, p. 2119–2162.

―――― and J. C. Freeman, 1953, Interrelations between jet behavior and hydraulic processes observed at deltaic river mouths and tidal inlets, Chap. 12 of J. W. Johnson, ed., 3d Coastal Engineering Conf. Proc., October 1952: p. 165–175.

―――― et al., 1959, World-wide evidence of deltas off the mouths of submarine canyons, in International Oceanography Congress Preprints: Am. Assoc. Adv. Sci., p. 595.

Beal, M. A., and F. P. Shepard, 1956, A use of roundness to determine depositional environments: Jour. Sed. Petrology, v. 27, p. 49–60.

Beall, A. O., Jr., 1968, Sedimentary processes operative along the western Louisiana shoreline: Jour. Sed. Petrology, v. 38, no. 3, p. 869–877.

Beerbower, J. R., and M. H. Hait, 1959, Silurian fish in northeastern Pennsylvania and northern New Jersey: Pennsylvania Acad. Sci. Proc., v. 33, p. 198–203.

Bernard, H. A., and R. J. LeBlanc, 1965, Resume of the Quaternary geology of the northwestern Gulf of Mexico province, in H. E. Wright, Jr., and D. G. Frey, eds., The Quaternary of the United States: Princeton, New Jersey, Princeton Univ. Press, p. 137–185.

―――― and C. F. Major, Jr., 1963, Recent meander belt deposits of the Brazos River: an alluvial "sand" model (abs.): Am. Assoc. Petroleum Geologists Bull., v. 47, no. 2, p. 350.

―――― R. J. LeBlanc, and C. F. Major, 1962, Recent and Pleistocene geology of southeast Texas, Field excursion no. 3, in Geology of the Gulf Coast and central Texas and guidebook of excursions, Geol. Soc. America, 1962 Ann. Mtg.: Houston, Texas, Houston Geol. Soc., p. 175–224.

―――― C. F. Major, Jr., and B. S. Parrott, 1959, The Galveston barrier island and environs: a model for predicting reservoir occurrence and trend: Gulf Coast Assoc. Geol. Socs. Trans., v. 9, p. 221–224.

―――― et al., 1970, Recent sediments of southeast Texas, a field guide to the Brazos alluvial and deltaic plains and the Galveston barrier island complex: Texas Univ. Bur. Econ. Geology Guidebook 11.

Beutner, E. C., L. A. Gleckinger, and T. M. Gard, 1967, Bedding geometry in a Pennsylvanian channel sandstone: Geol. Soc. America Bull., v. 78, no. 7, p. 911–916.

Blanton, S. L., 1963, Birth and death of an offshore bar: Gulf Coast Assoc. Geol. Socs. Trans., v. 13, p. 95–97.

Blench, T., 1951a, Hydraulics of sediment-bearing canals and rivers: Vancouver, British Columbia, Evans Industries, Ltd.

―――― 1951b, Regime theory for self-formed sediment-bearing channels: Am. Soc. Civil Engineers Proc., v. 77, separate 70, p. 1–18.

Bluck, B. J., 1967, Sedimentation of beach gravels: examples from South Wales: Jour. Sed. Petrology, v. 37, no. 1, p. 128–156.

Boyd, D. R., and B. F. Dyer, 1964, Frio barrier bar system of South Texas: Gulf Coast Assoc. Geol. Socs. Trans., v. 14, p. 309–322; 1965, South Texas Geol. Soc. Bull., v. 5, no. 4, p. 3–16.

Bradley, J. S., 1957, Differentiation of marine and subaerial sedimentary environments by volume percentage of heavy minerals, Mustang Island, Texas: Jour. Sed. Petrology, v. 27, p. 116–125.

Bradley, W. C., 1957, Origin of marine-terrace deposits in the Santa Cruz area, California: Geol. Soc. America Bull., v. 68, no. 4, p. 421–444.

Brown, L. F., Jr., 1969, Geometry and distribution of fluvial and deltaic sandstones (Pennsylvanian and Permian), north-central Texas: Gulf Coast Assoc. Geol. Socs. Trans., v. 19, p. 23–47.

Brune, G. M., 1950, Dynamic concept of sediment sources: Am. Geophys. Union Trans., v. 31, no. 4, p. 587–594.

Buckley, A. B., 1922–23, The influence of silt on the velocity of flowing water in open channels: Inst. Civil Engineers Proc., v. 216, p. 183–211.

Bullard, F. M., 1942, Source of beach and river sands on Gulf Coast of Texas: Geol. Soc. America Bull., v. 53, no. 7, p. 1021–1043.

Burnham, W. L., 1956, Sand studies, 14 to K interval, central Anzoategui, Venezuela: unpub. rept.

Busch, D. A., 1953, The significance of deltas in subsurface exploration: Tulsa Geol. Soc. Digest, v. 21, p. 71–80.

———— 1959, Prospecting for stratigraphic traps: Am. Assoc. Petroleum Geologists Bull., v. 43, no. 12, p. 2829–2843.

———— 1963, Methods of prospecting for stratigraphic oil and gas traps: Assoc. Française Tech. Pétrole Bull. 160, pt. 1, p. 459–464; Bull. 161, pt. 2, p. 633–643.

———— 1971, Genetic units in delta prospecting: Am. Assoc. Petroleum Geologists Bull., v. 55, no. 8, p. 1137–1154.

Byrne, J. V., D. O. LeRoy, and C. M. Riley, 1959, The chenier plain and its stratigraphy, southwestern Louisiana: Gulf Coast Assoc. Geol. Socs. Trans., v. 9, p. 1–23, 237–260.

Calvert, W. L., 1962, Sub-Trenton rocks from Lee County, Virginia, to Fayette County, Ohio: Ohio Div. Geol. Survey Rept. Inv. 45, 57 p.

———— 1963, Sub-Trenton rocks of Ohio in cross sections from West Virginia and Pennsylvania to Michigan: Ohio Div. Geol. Survey Rept. Inv. 49, 5 p.

Campbell, C. V., 1971, Depositional model— Upper Cretaceous Gallup beach shoreline, Shiprock area, northwestern New Mexico: Jour. Sed. Petrology, v. 41, no. 2, p. 395–409.

Cherry, J. A., 1966, Sand movement along equilibrium beaches north of San Francisco: Jour. Sed. Petrology, v. 36, no. 2, p. 341–357.

Choubert, B., 1948, Sur des phenomenes actuels de sedimentation le long des cots guyanaises: Acad. Sci. Comptes Rendus, v. 227.

Cobb, W. C., 1952, The passes of the Mississippi River: Am. Soc. Civil Engineers, Preprint 13, 23 p.

Coleman, J. M., 1966, Recent coastal sedimentation: central Louisiana coast: Louisiana State Univ. Coastal Studies Inst. Tech. Rept. 29, p. 1–73.

———— 1969, Brahmaputra River: channel processes and sedimentation: Sed. Geology, v. 3, no. 2–3, p. 131–239.

———— and S. M. Gagliano, 1964, Cyclic sedimentation in the Mississippi River deltaic plain: Louisiana State Univ. Coastal Studies Inst. Tech. Rept. 16, pt. G.; Gulf Coast Assoc. Geol. Socs. Trans., v. 14, p. 67–80.

———— et al., 1964, Minor sedimentary structures in a prograding distributary: Marine Geology, v. 1, p. 240–258.

Conatser, W. E., 1971, Grand Isle: a barrier island in the Gulf of Mexico: Geol. Soc. America Bull., v. 82, no. 11, p. 3049–3068.

Corbett, D. M., et al., 1943, Stream-gaging procedure: U.S. Geol. Survey Water-Supply Paper 888, 245 p.

Cotton, C. A., 1954, Deductive morphology and genetic classification of coasts: Sci. Monthly, v. 78, no. 3, p. 163–181.

Cross, W. P., and R. H. Bernhagen, 1949, Ohio stream-flow characteristics, Part I, flow duration: Ohio Dept. Nat. Resources Bull. 10, 40 p.

Curray, J. R., 1956, Dimensional grain orientation studies of recent coastal sands: Am. Assoc. Petroleum Geologists Bull., v. 40, no. 10, p. 2440–2456.

———— F. J. Emmel, and P. J. S. Crampton, 1969, Holocene history of a strand plain, Nayarit, Mexico, in A. A. Castañares and F. B Phleger, eds., Coastal lagoons, a symposium—UNAM-UNESCO, Mexico, D.F., 1967: Mexico, D.F., Univ. Nac. Autónoma México, p. 63–100.

Dapples, E. C., W. C. Krumbein, and L. L. Sloss, 1948, Tectonic control of lithologic associations: Am. Assoc. Petroleum Geologists Bull., v. 32, no. 10, p. 1924–1947.

Das, I., 1950, Theory of the flow of water and universal hydraulic diagrams: Jour. Central Board Irrigation (India), v. 7, no. 2, p. 151–162.

Davis, R. A., Jr., and W. T. Fox, 1972, Coastal processes and nearshore sand bars: Jour. Sed. Petrology, v. 42, no. 2, p. 401–412.

Davis, W. M., 1899, The geographical cycle: Geog. Jour., v. 14, p. 481–504.

———— 1902, Base-level, grade and peneplain: Jour. Geology, v. 10, p. 77–111.

Dillard, W. R., D. P. Oak, and N. W. Bass, 1941, Chanute oil pool, Neosho County, Kansas—a water-flooding operation, in A. I. Levorson, ed., Stratigraphic type oil fields: Tulsa, Oklahoma, Am. Assoc. Petroleum Geologists, p. 57–77.

Dodge, C. F., 1965, Genesis of an Upper Cretaceous offshore bar near Arlington, Texas: Jour. Sed. Petrology, v. 35, no. 1, p. 22–35.

Donaldson, A. C., 1967, Deltaic sands and sandstones, in Symposium on recently developed geologic principles and sedimentation of the Permo-Pennsylvanian of the Rocky Mountains: Wyoming Geol. Assoc. 20th Ann. Field Conf., Casper, Wyoming, 1966, Guidebook, p. 31–62h.

Doran, E., Jr., 1955, Land forms of the southeast Bahamas: Texas Univ. Pub. No. 5509, Dept. Geography, p. 1–38.

Duboul-Razavet, C., 1956, Contribution à l'étude géologique et sédimentologique du delta du

Rhône: Soc. Géol. France Mém. 76, v. 35, no. 3, 234 p.

—— and C. Kruit, 1957, Sédimentologie du delta du Rhône: Inst. Français Pétrole Rev., v. 12, no. 4, p. 399–410.

Dunbar, C. O., and J. Rodgers, 1957, Principles of stratigraphy: New York, John Wiley & Sons, 356 p. (especially p. 74–88, 137–140).

Einstein, H. A., 1950, The bed-load function for sediment transportation in open channel flow: U.S. Dept. Agriculture Tech. Bull. 1026.

—— and N. L. Barbarossa, 1951, River channel roughness: Am. Soc. Civil Engineers Proc., v. 77, p. 12.

Eisenstatt, P., 1960, Little Creek field, Lincoln and Pike Counties, Mississippi: Gulf Coast Assoc. Geol. Socs. Trans., v. 10, p. 206–213.

Élie de Beaumont, L., 1845, Leçons de géologie pratique: Paris, p. 223–252.

Ellison, W. D., 1945, Some effects of raindrops and surface-flow on soil erosion and infiltration: Am. Geophys. Union Trans., v. 26, no. 3, p. 415–430.

Evans, O. F., 1942, The origin of spits, bars and related structures: Jour. Geology, v. 50, no. 7, p. 846–965.

Fergusson, J., 1863, Delta of the Ganges: Geol. Soc. London Quart. Jour., v. 19, p. 321–354.

Fisher, J. J., 1968, Barrier island formation: discussion: Geol. Soc. America Bull., v. 79, no. 10, p. 1421–1426.

Fisher, W. L., and J. H. McGowen, 1967, Depositional systems in the Wilcox Group of Texas and their relationship to oil and gas: Gulf Coast Assoc. Geol. Socs. Trans., v. 17, p. 105–125.

—— and ——— 1969, Depositional systems in the Wilcox Group (Eocene) of Texas and their relationship to occurrence of oil and gas: Am. Assoc. Petroleum Geologists Bull., v. 53, no. 1, p. 30–54.

—— et al., 1969, Delta systems in the exploration for oil and gas, a research colloquium: Texas Univ. Bur. Econ. Geology, 78 p.

Fisk, H. N., 1944, Geological investigation of the alluvial valley of the lower Mississippi River: Vicksburg, Mississippi, U.S. Army Corps Engineers, Mississippi River Comm.

——— 1947, Fine-grained alluvial deposits and their effects on Mississippi River activity: Vicksburg, Mississippi, U.S. Army Corps Engineers, Mississippi River Comm.

——— 1948, Geological investigations of the lower Mermentau River basin and adjacent areas in coastal Louisiana: Vicksburg, Mississippi, U.S. Army Corps Engineers, Mississippi River Comm., p. 78.

——— 1952, Geological investigation of the Atchafalaya Basin and problems of Mississippi River diversion: Vicksburg, Mississippi, U.S. Army Corps Engineers, Mississippi River Comm., p. 1–145.

——— 1955, Sand facies of Recent Mississippi delta deposits: 4th World Petroleum Cong. Proc., Rome, 1955, sec. 1, p. 377–398.

——— 1959, Padre Island and the Laguna Madre flats, coastal south Texas, in R. J. Russell, chm., 2d Coastal Geography Conf., April 6–9: Louisiana State Univ. Coastal Studies Inst., p. 103–151.

——— 1960, Recent Mississippi River sedimentation and peat accumulation, in Ernest van Aelst, ed., 4th Congrès pour l'avancement des études de stratigraphie et de géologie du Carbonifère, Heerlen, Sept. 15–20: Compte Rendu, v. 1, p. 187–199.

——— 1961, Bar-finger sands of the Mississippi delta, in J. A. Peterson and J. C. Osmond, eds., Geometry of sandstone bodies: Tulsa, Oklahoma, Am. Assoc. Petroleum Geologists, p. 29–52.

——— and E. McFarlan, Jr., 1955, Late Quaternary deltaic deposits of the Mississippi River —local sedimentation and basin tectonics, in A. Poldervaart, ed., Crust of the earth, a symposium: Geol. Soc. America Spec. Paper 62, p. 279–302.

——— et al., 1954, Sedimentary framework of the modern Mississippi delta: Jour. Sed. Petrology, v. 24, no. 2, p. 76–99.

Flores, R. M., 1967, Relationship of geometry to the origin of the Lower Freeport sandstone (middle Allegheny) of eastern Ohio: Jour. Sed. Petrology, v. 37, no. 2, p. 624–632.

Folk, R. L., 1962, Of skewnesses and sands (disc.): Jour. Sed. Petrology, v. 32, p. 145–146.

—— and C. C. Mason, 1958, Differentiation of environments: Jour. Sed. Petrology, v. 28, no. 2, p. 211–226.

Frazier, D. E., 1967, Recent deltaic deposits of the Mississippi River: their development and chronology: Gulf Coast Assoc. Geol. Socs. Trans., v. 17, p. 287–315.

—— and A. Osanik, 1961, Point-bar deposits, Oil River locksite, Louisiana: Gulf Coast Assoc. Geol. Socs. Trans., v. 11, p. 121–137.

—— and ——— 1969, Recent peat deposits, Louisiana coastal plain, in Environments of coal deposition: Geol. Soc. America Spec. Paper 114, p. 63–85.

Friedman, G. M., 1961, Distinction between dune, beach, and river sands from their textural characteristics: Jour. Sed. Petrology, v. 31, p. 514–529.

——— 1967, Dynamic processes and statistical parameters compared for size frequency distribution of beach and river sands: Jour. Sed. Petrology, v. 37, no. 2, p. 327–354.

Friedman, S. A., 1960, Channel sandstones in the Middle Pennsylvanian rocks of Indiana: Indiana Geol. Survey Rept. Prog., no. 23, p. 59.

Galloway, W. E., and L. F. Brown, Jr., 1972, Depositional systems and shelf-slope relationships in Upper Pennsylvanian rocks, north-central Texas: Texas Univ. Bur. Econ. Geol. Rept. Inv. No. 75, 62 p.

Gary, M., R. McAfee, Jr., and C. L. Wolf, eds., 1972, Glossary of geology: Washington, D.C., Am. Geol. Inst., 805 p., bibliog. 52 p.

Geyskes, D. C., 1948, On the structure and origin of the sandy ridges in the coastal zone of Surinam: Koninkl. Nederlandsch Aardrijksk. Genoot. Tijdschr., v. 69, p. 15–237.

Gilbert, G. K., 1885, The topographic feature of lake shores: U.S. Geol. Survey 5th Ann. Rept., p. 69–123.

———— 1914, Transportation of debris by running water: U.S. Geol. Survey Prof. Paper 86, 263 p.

Glymph, L. M., 1951, Relation of sedimentation to accelerated erosion in the Missouri River basin: U.S. Dept. Agriculture Oil Consulting Service SCS-TP-120, p. 20.

Goldstein, A., Jr., 1942, Sedimentary petrologic provinces of the northern Gulf of Mexico: Jour. Sed. Petrology, v. 12, no. 2, p. 77–84.

Gould, H. R., 1972, Environmental indicators—a key to the stratigraphic record: Soc. Econ. Paleontologists and Mineralogists Spec. Pub. No. 16, p. 1–3.

———— and E. McFarlan, Jr., 1959, Geologic history of the chenier plain, southwestern Louisiana: Gulf Coast Assoc. Geol. Socs. Trans., v. 9, p. 261–270.

———— and J. P. Morgan, 1962, Coastal Louisiana swamps and marshlands, Field Trip No. 9 in Geology of the Gulf Coast and central Texas and guidebook of excursions, Geol. Soc. America 1962 Ann. Mtg.: Houston, Tex., Houston Geol. Soc., p. 287–341.

Grabau, A. W., 1909, The Medina and Shawangunk problems in Pennsylvania (abs.): Science, n.s., v. 30, p. 415.

———— 1913, Principles of stratigraphy: New York, 1185 p.; revised, 1924: New York, A. G. Seiler, 1185 p.; reprinted, 1960: New York, Dover Publications, 2 v., 1185 p. (especially p. 607–640).

Greenman, N. N., and R. J. LeBlanc, 1956, Recent marine sediments and environments of northwest Gulf of Mexico: Am. Assoc. Petroleum Geologists Bull., v. 40, no. 5, p. 813–847.

Gresswell, R. K., 1957, The physical geography of beaches and coastlines: London, Hulton Educational Publications.

Griffith, E. G., 1966, Geology of Saber bar, Logan and Weld Counties, Colorado: Am. Assoc. Petroleum Geologists Bull., v. 50, no. 10, p. 2112–2118.

Griffith, W. M., 1927, A theory of silt and scour: Inst. Civil Engineers Proc., v. 223.

Griggs, G. B., and L. D. Kulm, 1970, Sedimentation in Cascadia deep-sea channel: Geol. Soc. America Bull., v. 81, no. 5, p. 1361–1384.

Guilcher, A., 1958, Coastal and submarine morphology: New York, John Wiley & Sons, 274 p.

———— 1959, Coastal sand ridges and marshes and their environment near Grand Popo and Ouidah, Dahomey, in R. J. Russell, chm., 2d Coastal Geography Conf., April 6–9: Louisiana State Univ. Coastal Studies Inst., p. 189–212.

Guillou, R. B., and J. J. Glass, 1957, A reconnaissance study of the beach sands of Puerto Rico: U.S. Geol. Survey Bull. 1042-I, p. 273–305.

Halbouty, M. T., 1967, Hidden trends and features: Gulf Coast Assoc. Geol. Socs. Trans., v. 17, p. 2–23.

———— and T. D. Barber, 1961, Port Acres and Port Arthur fields, Jefferson County, Texas: Gulf Coast Assoc. Geol. Socs. Trans., v. 11, p. 225–234.

Hammond, E. H., 1954, A geomorphic study of the Cape region of Baja, California: California Univ. Pubs. Geography, v. 10, p. 45–112.

Hedgpeth, J. W., 1947, The Laguna Madre of Texas: 12th North American Wildlife Conference Trans., p. 364–380.

Hembree, C. H., et al., 1952, Sedimentation and chemical quality of water in the Powder River drainage basin, Wyoming and Montana: U.S. Geol. Survey Circ. 170, v, 92 p.

Hobday, D. K., and J. G. Reading, 1972, Fair weather versus storm processes in shallow marine sand bar sequences in the late Precambrian of Finnmark, north Norway: Jour. Sed. Petrology, v. 42, no. 2, p. 318–324.

Holle, C. G., 1952, Sedimentation at the mouth of the Mississippi River, Chap. 10 of J. W. Johnson, ed., 2d Coastal Engineering. Conf. Proc., November 1951: p. 111–129.

Hollenshead, C. T., and R. L. Pritchard, 1961, Geometry of producing Mesaverde sandstones, San Juan basin, in J. A. Peterson and J. C. Osmond, eds., Geometry of sandstone bodies: Tulsa, Oklahoma, Am. Assoc. Petroleum Geologists, p. 98–118.

Hopkins, M. E., 1958, Geology and petrology of the Anvil Rock Sandstone of southern Illinois: Illinois Geol. Survey Circ. 256, 49 p.

Horton, R. E., 1945, Erosional development of streams and their drainage basins—hydrophysical approach to quantitative morphology: Geol. Soc. America Bull., v. 56, no. 3, p. 275–370.

Hoskins, D. M., 1961, Stratigraphy and paleontology of the Bloomsburg Formation of Pennsylvania and adjacent states: Pennsylvania Geol. Survey Bull. G36, 4th ser., 125 p.

———— and R. R. Conlin, 1958, Invertebrate fossils from the Bloomsburg Formation of central Pennsylvania: Pennsylvania Acad. Sci. Proc., v. 32, p. 156–161.

Howe, H. V., et al., 1935, Physiography of coastal southwest Louisiana; reports on the geology of Cameron and Vermilion Parishes: Louisiana Geol. Survey Geol. Bull., no. 6, p. 1–72.

Howell, J. V., chm., 1960, Glossary of geology and related sciences: Washington, D.C., Am. Geol. Inst., 325 p.; Supplement, 72 p.

Hoyt, J. H., 1967, Barrier island formation: Geol. Soc. America Bull., v. 78, no. 9, p. 1125–1136.

———— 1968, Barrier island formation: reply: Geol. Soc. America Bull., v. 79, no. 10, p. 1427–1432.

———— 1970, Development and migration of barrier islands, north Gulf of Mexico: discussion: Geol. Soc. America Bull., v. 81, no. 12, p. 3779–3782.

———— and V. J. Henry, Jr., 1965, Significance of inlet sedimentation in the recognition of ancient barrier islands, in Sedimentation of Late Cretaceous and Tertiary outcrops, Rock

Springs uplift: Wyoming Geol. Assoc. 19th Field Conf., Casper, Wyoming, 1965, Guidebook, p. 190–194.

—— and —— 1967, Influence of island migration on barrier island sedimentation: Geol. Soc. America Bull., v. 78, no. 1, p. 77–86.

—— R. J. Weimer, and V. J. Henry, Jr., 1964, Late Pleistocene and recent sedimentation, central Georgia coast, U.S.A., in Developments in sedimentology, v. 1, Deltaic and shallow marine deposits: 6th Internat. Sedimentological Cong., Amsterdam and Antwerp, 1963, Proc., p. 170–176.

—— et al., 1952, Geologic history and development of the barrier islands in the vicinity of Sapelo Island, Georgia (abs.): Southeastern Section Geol. Soc. America Mtg., April 13, 1952.

Hoyt, W. V., 1959, Erosional channel in the middle Wilcox near Yoakum, Lavaca County, Texas: Gulf Coast Assoc. Geol. Socs. Trans., v. 9, p. 41–50.

Johnson, D. W., 1919, Shore processes and shoreline development: New York, John Wiley & Sons, 584 p.

—— 1925, The New England-Acadian shoreline: New York, John Wiley & Sons, 608 p.

Johnson, J. W., 1943, Laboratory investigations on bed-load transportation and bed roughness: U.S. Soil Conserv. Service Tech. Pub. 50.

Johnson, K. G., and G. M. Friedman, 1969, The Tully clastic correlatives (Upper Devonian) of New York State: a model for recognition of alluvial, dune (?), tidal, nearshore (bar and lagoon), and offshore sedimentary environments in a tectonic delta complex: Jour. Sed. Petrology, v. 39, no. 2, p. 451–485.

Johnson, W. H., 1921, Sedimentation of the Fraser River delta: Canada Geol. Survey Mem. 125, p. 46.

—— 1922, The character of the stratification of the sediments in the recent delta of the Fraser River, British Columbia, Canada: Jour. Geology, v. 30, p. 115–129.

Jordan, L., 1957, Subsurface stratigraphic names of Oklahoma: Okla. Geol. Survey Guidebook 6, 220 p.

Keller, W. D., 1945, Size distribution of sand in some dunes, beaches, and sandstones: Am. Assoc. Petroleum Geologists Bull., v. 29, p. 215–221.

Kennedy, R. G., 1895, Prevention of silting in irrigation canals: Inst. Civil Engineers Proc., v. 119, p. 281–290.

Kerr, R. D., and J. O. Nigra, 1952, Eolian sand control: Am. Assoc. Petroleum Geologists Bull., v. 36, pt. 2, p. 1541–1573.

Khaiwka, M. H., 1968, Geometry and depositional environments of Pennsylvanian reservoir sandstones, northwestern Oklahoma: Univ. Oklahoma, Ph.D. thesis, 126 p.

—— 1973, Geometry and depositional environment of Morrow reservoir sandstones, northwestern Oklahoma: Shale Shaker, v. 23, no. 9, p. 196–214; v. 23, no. 10, p. 228–232.

Kholief, M. M., E. Hilmy, and A. Shahat, 1969, Geological and mineralogical studies of some

sand deposits in the Nile delta, U.A.R.: Jour. Sed. Petrology, v. 39, no. 4, p. 1520–1529.

King, C. A. M., 1959, Beaches and coasts: London, E. Arnold.

Klenova, M. V., 1959, Regularities in formation of delta sediments and relief (lithomorphogenesis) [abs.]: 1st Internat. Oceanography Cong., Preprints, p. 630–634 (Engl. summary).

Kolb, C. R., and J. R. Van Lopik, 1966, Depositional environments of the Mississippi River deltaic plain, southeastern Louisiana, in Deltas in their geological framework: Houston, Texas, Houston Geol. Soc., p. 17–61.

Kruit, C., 1955, Sediments of the Rhône delta; I, Grain size and microfauna: Koninkl. Nederlandsch Geol.-Mijnb. Genoot., Verh., Geol. Ser., v. 15, p. 357–499.

Krumbein, W. C., 1945, Sedimentary maps and oil exploration: New York Acad. Sci. Trans., ser. 2, v. 7, no. 7, p. 159–166.

—— 1948, Lithofacies maps and regional sedimentary-stratigraphic analysis: Am. Assoc. Petroleum Geologists Bull., v. 32, no. 10, p. 1909–1923.

Kuenen, Ph. H., 1950, Marine geology: New York, John Wiley & Sons, 568 p.

—— 1959, Dutch post-war coastal studies, in R. J. Russell, chm., 2d Coastal Geography Conf., April 6–9: Louisiana State Univ. Coastal Studies Inst., p. 285–300.

Kuwahiro, I., 1958, Morphological studies on alluvial plains in Setouchi district: Geog. Rev. Japan, v. 31, no. 3, p. 160–168.

Lacey, G., 1930, Stable channels in alluvium: Inst. Civil Engineers Proc., v. 229, pt. 1, p. 259–384.

—— 1939, Regime flow in incoherent alluvium: Simla, Central Board Irrigation (India) Pub. 20.

Lagaaij, R., and F. P. H. W. Kopstein, 1964, Typical features on a fluviomarine offlap sequence, in Developments in sedimentology, v. 1, Deltaic and shallow marine deposits: 6th Internat. Sedimentological Cong. Proc., v. 1, p. 216–226.

Lahee, F. H., 1941, Field geology: New York, McGraw-Hill, 853 p. (especially p. 80–83).

Lane, D. W., 1963, Sedimentary environments in Cretaceous Dakota Sandstone in northwestern Colorado: Am. Assoc. Petroleum Geologists Bull., v. 47, no. 2, p. 229–256.

Lane, E. W., 1937, Stable channels in erodible materials: Am. Soc. Civil Engineers Trans., no. 102, p. 123–194.

—— and W. M. Borland, 1951, Estimating bed-load: Am. Geophys. Union Trans., v. 32, no. 1, p. 121–123.

Lara, J. M., and C. R. Miller, 1951, Conveyance channel widening study, Middle Rio Grande Project: U.S. Bur. Reclamation Open-File Rept.

Leatherock, C., 1937, Physical characteristics of Bartlesville and Burbank sands in northeastern Oklahoma and southeastern Kansas: Am. Assoc. Petroleum Geologists Bull., v. 21, p. 246–258.

LeBlanc, R. J., and W. D. Hodgson, 1959a, Origin and development of the Texas shoreline, *in* R. J. Russell, chm., 2d Coastal Geography Conf., April 6–9: Louisiana State Univ. Coastal Studies Inst., p. 57–101.

———— and ———— 1959b, Origin and development of the Texas shoreline: Gulf Coast Assoc. Geol. Socs. Trans., v. 9, p. 197–220.

———— and ———— 1961, Origin and development of the Texas shoreline, *in* Symposium on Late Cretaceous rocks, Wyoming and adjacent areas: Wyoming Geol. Assoc. 16th Ann. Field Conf., Casper, Wyoming, 1961, p. 253–275.

Leontyev, O. K., and L. G. Nikiforov, 1966, An approach to the problem of the origin of barrier bars: 2d Internat. Oceanographic Cong., Abs. of Papers, p. 221–222.

Leopold, L. B., and T. Maddock, Jr., 1953, The hydraulic geometry of stream channels and some physiographic implications: U.S. Geol. Survey Prof. Paper 252, 57 p.

Lindley, E. S., 1919, Regime channels: Punjab Eng. Cong. Proc., v. 7.

Lins, T. W., 1950, Origin and environment of the Tonganoxie sandstone in northeastern Kansas: Kansas Geol. Survey Bull. 86, pt. 5, p. 105–140.

Linsley, R. K., *et al.*, 1949, Applied hydrology: New York, McGraw-Hill, 689 p.

Lohse, E. A., 1955, Dynamic geology of the modern coastal region, northwest Gulf of Mexico, *in* J. L. Hough and H. W. Menard, eds., Finding ancient shorelines, a symposium: Soc. Econ. Paleontologists and Mineralogists Spec. Pub. No. 3, p. 99–105.

Lowman, S. W., 1949, Sedimentary facies in Gulf Coast: Am. Assoc. Petroleum Geologists Bull., v. 33, no. 12, p. 1939–1997.

Lynch, S. A., 1954, Geology of the Gulf of Mexico, *in* Chap. 2 *of* Gulf of Mexico—its origin, waters, and marine life: U.S. Fish and Wildlife Service Fishery Bull. 89, p. 67–86.

Macklin, J. H., 1948, Concept of the graded river: Geol. Soc. America Bull., v. 59, p. 463–512.

Martin, R., 1966, Paleogeomorphology and its application to exploration for oil and gas (with examples from Western Canada): Am. Assoc. Petroleum Geologists Bull., v. 50, no. 10, p. 2277–2311.

McCurdy, P. G., 1947, Manual of coastal delineation from aerial photographs: Washington, D.C., U.S. Hydrographic Office, 143 p.

McEwen, M. C., 1963, Sedimentary facies of the Trinity River delta, Texas: Houston, Texas, Rice Univ., unpub. thesis.

McGill, J. T., 1959, Coastal classification maps —a review, *in* R. J. Russell, chm., 2d Coastal Geography Conf., April 6–9: Louisiana State Univ. Coastal Studies Inst., p. 1–21; summary, 1958: Geog. Rev., v. 48, no. 3, p. 402–405.

McGowen, J. H., 1970, Gum Hollow fan delta, Nueces Bay, Texas: Texas Univ. Bur. Econ. Geology Rept. Inv. 69.

McKee, E. D., 1957, Flume experiments on the production of stratification and cross-stratification: Jour. Sed. Petrology, v. 27, no. 2, p. 129–134.

———— and T. S. Sterrett, 1961, Laboratory experiments on form and structure of longshore bars and beaches, *in* J. A. Peterson and J. C. Osmond, eds., Geometry of sandstone bodies: Tulsa, Oklahoma, Am. Assoc. Petroleum Geologists, p. 13–28.

Miller, D. N., Jr., 1962, Patterns of barrier bar sedimentation and its similarity to Lower Cretaceous Fall River stratigraphy, *in* Symposium on Early Cretaceous rocks of Wyoming and adjacent areas: Wyoming Geol. Assoc. 17th Ann. Field Conf., Casper, Wyoming, 1962, p. 232–247.

Morgan, J. P., 1951, Report on the mudlumps at the mouths of the Mississippi River; Part I, The occurrence and origin of the mudlumps at the mouths of the Mississippi River: New Orleans District, U.S. Army Corps Engineers, unpub. rept., 127 p.

———— and P. B. Larimore, 1957, Changes in the Louisiana shoreline: Gulf Coast Assoc. Geol. Socs. Trans., v. 17, p. 303–310.

———— and R. H. Shaver, 1970, Deltaic sedimentation, modern and ancient: Soc. Econ. Paleontologists and Mineralogists Spec. Pub. No. 15.

———— *et al.*, 1968, Mudlumps—diapiric structures in Mississippi delta sediments, *in* J. Braunstein and G. D. O'Brien, eds., Diapirism and diapirs, a symposium: Am. Assoc. Petroleum Geologists Mem. 8, p. 145–161.

Mothersill, J. S., 1969, A grain size analysis of longshore-bars and troughs, Lake Superior, Ontario: Jour. Sed. Petrology, v. 39, no. 4, p. 1317–1324.

Muller, J., 1959, Palynology of Recent Orinoco delta and shelf sediments; Reports of the Orinoco shelf expedition, v. 5: Micropaleontology, v. 5, no. 1, p. 1–32.

Nanz, R. N., 1954, Genesis of Oligocene sandstone reservoir, Seeligson field, Jim Wells and Kleberg Counties, Texas: Am. Assoc. Petroleum Geologists Bull., v. 38, no. 1, p. 96–117.

Nota, D. J. G., 1958, Sediments of the western Guiana shelf: Utrecht Univ. dissert., 98 p.; Wageningen, H. Veenman & Zonen; Landbouwhogeschool, Med. 58 (2).

Oomkens, E., 1967, Depositional sequences and sand distribution in a deltaic complex; a sedimentological investigation of the post-glacial Rhône delta complex: Geologie en Mijnbouw, v. 46, no. 7, p. 265–278.

Otvos, E. G., Jr., 1970a, Development and migration of barrier islands, northern Gulf of Mexico: Geol. Soc. American Bull., v. 81, no. 1, p. 241–246.

———— 1970b, Development and migration of barrier islands, north Gulf of Mexico: reply: Geol. Soc. America Bull., v. 81, no. 12, p. 3783–3788.

Pepper, J. F., W. R. de Witt, Jr., and D. F. Demarest, 1954, Geology of the Bedford shale and Berea sandstone in the Appalachian basin: U.S. Geol. Survey Prof. Paper 259, 111 p.

———— *et al.*, 1944, Map of the Second Berea sand in Gallia, Meigs, Athens, Morgan, and Muskingum Counties, Ohio: U.S. Geol. Survey

Oil and Gas Inv. Prelim. Map 5.

—— et al., 1955, Geology of the Bedford shale and the Berea sandstone in the Appalachian basin: U.S. Geol. Survey Prof. Paper 259, p. 111.

Peterson, J. A., and J. C. Osmond, eds., 1961, Geometry of sandstone bodies: Tulsa, Oklahoma, Am. Assoc. Petroleum Geologists, 240 p.

Phleger, F. B, and G. C. Ewing, 1962, Sedimentology and oceanography of coastal lagoons in Baja California, Mexico: Geol. Soc. America Bull., v. 73, no. 2, p. 145–181.

Pincus, H. J., 1959, Type features of the Ohio shoreline of Lake Erie: Am. Soc. Civil Engineers Proc., Jour. Waterways and Harbors Div., v. 85, Paper 2297, no. WW4, p. 1–27.

—— 1960, Engineering geology of the Ohio shoreline of Lake Erie: Ohio Div. Shore Erosion Tech. Rept. 7.

Potter, P. E., 1962a, Shape and distribution pattern of Pennsylvanian sand bodies in Illinois: Illinois Geol. Survey Circ. 339, p. 35.

—— 1962b, Late Mississippian sandstones of Illinois: Illinois Geol. Survey Circ. 340, p. 36.

—— and F. J. Pettijohn, 1963, Paleocurrents and basin analysis: New York, Academic Press, 296 p.

Powers, W. E., 1958, Geomorphology of the Lake Michigan shoreline, final report: Northwestern Univ. Dept. Geography ONR Contract Nonr-1228(07), p. 1–103.

Price, W. A., 1951, Barrier island, not "offshore bar": Science, v. 113, no. 2939, p. 487–488.

—— 1954a, Correlation of shoreline type with offshore conditions in the Gulf of Mexico, in R. J. Russell, chm., 2d Coastal Geography Conf., April 6–9: Louisiana State Univ. Coastal Studies Inst., p. 11–30.

—— 1954b, Shoreline and coasts of the Gulf of Mexico, in Chap. 2 of Gulf of Mexico—its origin, waters, and marine life: U.S. Fish and Wildlife Service Fishery Bull. 89, v. 55, p. 39–65.

—— 1955, Environment and formation of the chenier plain: Quaternaria, v. 2, p. 75–86.

—— 1963, Patterns of flow and channeling in tidal inlets: Jour. Sed. Petrology, v. 33, no. 2, p. 279–290.

Pugh, J. C., 1953, The Porto Novo-Badagri sand ridge complex: Univ. Coll. Ibadan, Nigeria, Dept. Geography Research Notes, no. 3, p. 3–14.

Rainwater, E. H., 1963a, Stratigraphy and its role in the future exploration for oil and gas in the Gulf Coast: Gulf Coast Assoc. Geol. Socs. Trans., v. 13, p. 33–75.

—— 1963b, The environmental control of oil and gas occurrence in terrigenous clastic rocks: Gulf Coast Assoc. Geol. Socs. Trans., v. 13, p. 79–94.

Reineck, H. E., 1967, Layered sediments in tidal flats, beaches, and shelf bottoms of the North Sea, in Estuaries: Am. Assoc. Adv. Sci. Pub. 83, p. 191–206.

Rich, J. L., 1923, Shoestring sands of eastern Kansas: Am. Assoc. Petroleum Geologists Bull., v. 7, p. 103–113.

Rubey, W. W., 1933, Equilibrium conditions in debris-laden streams: Am. Geophys. Union Trans., 14th Ann. Mtg., p. 497–505.

—— 1952, Geology and mineral resources of Hardin and Brussels quadrangles (in Illinois): U.S. Geol. Survey Prof. Paper 218, v, 179 p.

Russell, R. J., 1936, Physiography of the lower Mississippi River delta, in Reports on the geology of Plaquemines and St. Bernard Parishes: Louisiana Dept. Conserv. Geol. Bull. 8, p. 3–193.

—— and H. V. Howe, 1935, Cheniers of southwestern Louisiana: Geog. Review, v. 25, p. 449–461.

—— and R. D. Russell, 1939, Mississippi River delta sedimentation, in P. D. Trask, ed., Recent marine sediments: Tulsa, Oklahoma, Am. Assoc. Petroleum Geologists, p. 153–177.

Sabins, F. F., Jr., 1963, Anatomy of stratigraphic trap, Bisti field, New Mexico: Am. Assoc. Petroleum Geologists Bull., v. 47, no. 2, p. 193–228.

Samojlov, I. V., 1956, Die Flussmündungen: Gotha, Hermann Haack, 647 p.

Schlee, J. S., and R. H. Moench, 1961, Properties and genesis of "Jackpile" sandstone, Laguna, New Mexico, in J. A. Petersen and J. C. Osmond, eds., Geometry of sandstone bodies: Tulsa, Oklahoma, Am. Assoc. Petroleum Geologists, p. 134–150.

Schumm, S. A., 1972, River morphology: Stroudsburg, Pennsylvania, Dowden, Hutchinson & Ross, 448 p.

—— and H. R. Khan, 1972, Experimental study of channel patterns: Geol. Soc. America Bull., v. 83, no. 6, p. 1755–1770.

Schwartz, M. L., 1972, Spits and bars: Stroudsburg, Pennsylvania, Dowden, Hutchinson & Ross, 464 p.

Scruton, P. C., 1960, Delta building and the deltaic sequence, in F. P. Shepard et al., eds., Recent sediments, northwest Gulf of Mexico: Tulsa, Oklahoma, Am. Assoc. Petroleum Geologists, p. 82–102.

Serra, E. F., III, 1950, Progress report—investigations of fluvial sediments of the Niobrara River near Cody, Nebraska: U.S. Geol. Survey Circ. 67, 25 p.

—— 1951, Measurement of bed-load sediment: Am. Geophys. Union Trans., v. 32, p. 123–126.

Shepard, F. P., 1937, Revised classification of marine shorelines: Jour. Geology, v. 45, p. 602–624.

—— 1948, Submarine geology: New York, Harper & Brothers, 348 p.

—— 1950a, Longshore-bars and longshore-troughs: Beach Erosion Board Tech. Memo, no. 15, 32 p.

—— 1950b, Submarine topography of the Gulf of California, Pt. 3 of 1940 E. W. Scripps cruise to the Gulf of California: Geol. Soc. America Mem. 43, 32 p.

—— 1952, Revised nomenclature for depositional coastal features: Am. Assoc. Petroleum Geologists Bull., v. 36, no. 10, p. 1902–1912.

———— and D. G. Moore, 1955a, Sediment zones bordering the barrier islands of central Texas coast, *in* J. L. Hough and H. W. Menard, eds., Finding ancient shorelines, a symposium: Soc. Econ. Paleontologists and Mineralogists Spec. Pub. No. 3, p. 78–98.

———— and ———— 1955b, Central Texas coast sedimentation: characteristics of sedimentary environments, recent history, and diagenesis: Am. Assoc. Petroleum Geologists Bull., v. 39, no. 8, p. 1463–1593.

Sherrill, R. E., P. A. Dickey, and L. S. Matteson, 1941, Types of stratigraphic oil pools in Venango sands of northwestern Pennsylvania, *in* A. I. Levorsen, ed., Stratigraphic type oil fields, a symposium: Tulsa, Oklahoma, Am. Assoc. Petroleum Geologists, p. 507–538.

Shulits, S., 1941, Rational equation of river-bed profile: Am. Geophys. Union Trans., 22d Ann. Mtg., pt. 3, p. 622–630.

Siever, R., 1951, The Mississippian-Pennsylvanian unconformity in southern Illinois: Am. Assoc. Petroleum Geologists Bull., v. 35, no. 3, p. 542–581; reprinted as Illinois Geol. Survey Rept. Inv. 152.

Steinmetz, R., 1972, Sedimentation of an Arkansas River sand bar in Oklahoma: a cautionary note on dipmeter interpretation: Shale Shaker, v. 23, no. 2, p. 32–38.

Stevens, J. C., 1937, Discussion *of* E. W. Lane, Stable channels in erodible materials: Am. Soc. Civil Engineers Trans., no. 102, p. 145–149.

Sverdrup, H. U., M. W. Johnson, and R. H. Fleming, 1942, The oceans, their physics, chemistry, and general biology: New York, Prentice-Hall, 1087 p.

Swann, D. H., 1964, Late Mississippian rhythmic sediments of Mississippi Valley: Am. Assoc. Petroleum Geologists Bull., v. 48, no. 5, p. 637–658.

Sykes, G. G., 1937, The Colorado delta: Carnegie Inst. Washington Pub. 460, 193 p.

Thomas, A. R., 1946, Slope formulas for rivers and canals: Jour. Central Board Irrigation (India), v. 3, no. 1, p. 40–49.

———— 1949, Analysis of hydraulic data of some boulder rivers: Jour. Central Board Irrigation (India), v. 6, no. 1, p. 67–71.

Thompson, W. O., 1937, Original structures of beaches, bars and dunes: Geol. Soc. America Bull., v. 48, no. 6, p. 723–751.

———— 1949, Lyons sandstone of Colorado Front Range: Am. Assoc. Petroleum Geologists Bull., v. 33, no. 1, p. 52–72.

Tinler, K. J., 1971, Active valley meanders in south-central Texas and their wider implications: Geol. Soc. America Bull., v. 82, no. 7, p. 1783–1800.

Todd, T. W., 1968, Dynamic diversion: Influence of longshore current-tidal flow interaction on chenier and barrier island plains: Jour. Sed. Petrology, v. 38, no. 3, p. 734–746.

Trowbridge, A. C., 1930, Building of Mississippi delta: Am. Assoc., Petroleum Geologists Bull., v. 14, no. 7, p. 867–901.

Twenhofel, W. H., 1926, Treatise on sedimenta-tion: Baltimore, Williams & Wilkins, 661 p.; reprinted 1961, New York, Dover Publications, 2 v., 926 p. (especially p. 836–850).

U.S. Army Corps of Engineers, 1935, Studies of river bed materials and their movement, with special references to the lower Mississippi River: U.S. Army Corps Engineers Waterways Expt. Sta. Misc. Paper 17, 161 p.

U.S. Bureau of Reclamation, 1949, Report of river control work and investigations, lower Colorado River basin, calendar year 1948 and 1949, Boulder City, Nevada: U.S. Bur. Reclamation Open-File Rept., 124 p.

U.S. Congress, 1953, Gulf shore of Galveston Island, Texas: Beach Erosion Control Study, House Doc. 218, 83d Cong., 1st Sess.

van Andel, T. H., 1955, Sediments of the Rhône delta, II, Sources and deposition of heavy minerals: Koninkl. Nederlandsch Geol.-Mijnb. Genoot., Verh., Geol. Ser., v. 15, p. 515–556.

———— 1967, The Orinoco delta: Jour. Sed. Petrology, v. 37, no. 2, p. 297–310.

———— *et al.*, 1954, Recent sediments of the Gulf of Paria: Reports of the Orinoco shelf expedition, v. 1: Koninkl. Nederlandse Akad. Wetensch. Proc., v. 20, no. 5, 238 p.

van de Graaf, F. R., 1972, Fluvial-deltaic facies of the Castlegate sandstone (Cretaceous), east-central Utah: Jour. Sed. Petrology, v. 42, no. 3, p. 558–571.

van Straaten, L. M. J. U., 1953, Rhythmic patterns on Dutch North Sea beaches: Geologie en Mijnbouw, v. 15, no. 3, p. 31–43.

———— 1954, Composition and structure of recent marine sediments in the Netherlands: Leidse Geol. Med., pt. 19, p. 1–96.

———— 1957, Recent sandstones on the coasts of the Netherlands and of the Rhône delta: Geologie en Mijnbouw, v. 19, p. 196–213.

———— 1959, Littoral and submarine morphology of the Rhône delta, *in* R. J. Russell, chm., 2d Coastal Geography Conf., April 6–9: Louisiana State Univ. Coastal Studies Inst., p. 233–264.

———— 1965, Coastal barrier deposits in south- and north-Holland, in particular in the areas around Scheveningen and Ijmuiden: Netherlands Geol. Stichting, Med., n.s., no. 17, p. 41–75.

Vanoni, V. A., 1941, Some experiments on the transportation of suspended load: Am. Geophys. Union Trans., 22d Ann Mtg., pt. 3, p. 608–620.

———— 1946, Transportation of suspended sediment by water: Am. Soc. Civil Engineers Trans., no. 111, p. 67–133.

Vann, J. H., 1959, The geomorphology of the Guiana coast, *in* R. J. Russell, chm., 2d Coastal Geography Conf., April 6–9: Louisiana State Univ. Coastal Studies Inst., p. 153–187.

Vice, R. B., and E. F. Serra, III, 1950, Progress report, investigations of fluvial sediments, Middle Loup River near Dunning and Milburn, Nebraska: U.S. Geol. Survey Open-File Rept.

von Englehardt, W., 1940, Die Unterscheidung wasser- und windsortierter Sande auf Grund der Korngrössenverteilung ihrer leichten und schweren Gemengteile: Chemie der Erde, v. 12, no. 4, p. 445–465.

von Engeln, O. D., and K. E. Caster, 1952, Geology: New York, McGraw-Hill, 730 p.

Wanek, A. A., 1954, Geologic map of the Mesa Verde area, Montezuma County, Colorado: U.S. Geol. Survey Oil and Gas Inv. Map OM152, scale 1:63,360.

Wanless, H. R., 1931, Pennsylvanian cycles in western Illinois: Illinois Geol. Survey Bull., v. 60, p. 179–193.

———— and J. M. Weller, 1932, Regional persistence of Pennsylvanian cycles (abs.): Geol. Soc. America Bull., v. 43, no. 1, p. 139.

Weimer, R. J., 1961, Upper Cretaceous delta on tectonic foreland, northern Colorado and southern Wyoming (abs.): Am. Assoc. Petroleum Geologists Bull., v. 45, no. 3, p. 417.

Weirich, T. E., 1953, Shelf principle of oil origin, migration and accumulation: Am. Assoc. Petroleum Geologists Bull., v. 37, p. 2027–2045.

Welder, F. A., 1959, Processes of deltaic sedimentation in the lower Mississippi River: Louisiana State Univ. Coastal Studies Inst. Tech. Rept. No. 12, p. 1–90.

Weller, J. M., 1930, Cyclical sedimentation of the Pennsylvanian period and its significance: Jour. Geology, v. 38, no. 2, p. 97–135.

———— 1956, Environment and history in identification of shoreline types: Quaternaria, v. 3, p. 151–166.

Willard, B., 1928, The age and origin of the Shawangunk formation: Jour. Paleontology, v. 1, no. 4, p. 255–258.

Wilson, C. W., Jr., 1948, Channels and channel-filling sediments of Richmond age in south-central Tennessee: Geol. Soc. America Bull., v. 59, no. 8, p. 733–765.

Yeakel, L. S., Jr., 1962, Tuscarora, Juniata, Bald Eagle paleocurrents and paleogeography in the central Appalachians: Geol. Soc. America Bull., v. 73, p. 1515–1540.

Zenkovich, V. P., 1962, Some new exploration results about sand shore development during the sea transgression: De Ingenieur, no. 17, Bouw en Waterbouwkunde, 9, p. 113–121.

index

The following index is a computerized KWIC (keyword in context) index. To locate a reference, the reader should begin by thinking of the significant words. He then should look in the index for the keyword entry for each of those words. The reference codes will direct him to the pages.

The columns on the right-hand side of the keyword index give the page number and a code number (1 or 3) indicating the nature of the source. The code is:

(1) for phrase from title; and

(3) for phrase from text, table, figure, or figure caption.

The keyword for each entry is located at the left-hand side of the page. The ($>$) sign indicates the first word in each title or key phrase. The ($<$) sign indicates the end of the title or key phrase.